TRACING YOUR ROMAN CATHOLIC ANCESTORS

FAMILY HISTORY FROM PEN & SWORD

TRACING YOUR ROMAN CATHOLIC ANCESTORS

A Guide for Family and Local Historians

Stuart A. Raymond

Pen & Sword
FAMILY HISTORY

First published in Great Britain in 2018
PEN & SWORD FAMILY HISTORY
an imprint of
Pen & Sword Books Ltd
47 Church Street
Barnsley, South Yorkshire, S70 2AS

Copyright © Stuart A. Raymond, 2018

ISBN 978 1 52671 668 2

Typeset in Palatino and Optima by CHIC GRAPHICS

Printed and bound in England by
TJ International Ltd, Padstow, Cornwall

Pen & Sword Books Ltd incorporates the imprints of Pen & Sword
Airworld, Archaeology, Atlas, Aviation, Battleground, Discovery, Family
History, Fiction, History, Maritime, Military, Military Classics, Politics,
Select, Social History, True Crime, Frontline Books, Leo Cooper,
Remember When, Seaforth Publishing, The Praetorian Press,
Wharncliffe Local History, Wharncliffe Transport,
Wharncliffe True Crime and White Owl.

For a complete list of Pen & Sword titles please contact
PEN & SWORD BOOKS LTD
47 Church Street, Barnsley, South Yorkshire, S70 2AS, England
E-mail: enquiries@pen-and-sword.co.uk
Website: www.pen-and-sword.co.uk

CONTENTS

ACKNOWLEDGEMENTS

My major debt in writing this book is to the authors whose works I have cited. I am grateful to the librarians at Trowbridge, Wiltshire & Swindon History Centre, Sarum College, Downside Abbey and the Bodleian Library for their assistance. Mark O'Meara has read my text, made many useful comments and saved me from many errors. I am also grateful to Simon Fowler for his assistance. Those errors that remain are of course my responsibility.

INTRODUCTION

Until the Reformation, the entire population of England and Wales were Roman Catholics. Under Edward VI, many became Protestants, and some went into exile when Queen Mary restored Catholicism. They returned to create a Protestant church when Elizabeth came to the throne in 1558. However, under Mary, others had deepened their Catholic faith. This particularly applied to her bishops. They remembered what had happened when their Henrician predecessors accepted the original breach with Rome, and, at great cost to themselves, declined to accept a fresh breach.

Under Elizabeth and subsequent monarchs, the number of Catholics dwindled, and remained small for several centuries. Rapid growth did not recommence until the huge expansion in Irish migration in the nineteenth century. Today, the Roman Catholic church is one of the most important Christian denominations in England and Wales.

This history means that most Catholics of the present generation are unlikely to be able to trace their Catholic ancestors for more than a few generations, or that the local historian will be able to trace a particular Catholic congregation back to the Reformation (although such congregations do exist). Conversely, it is quite possible that Protestants could trace Catholic ancestors from the sixteenth and seventeenth century. Mostly, the researcher is likely to be tracing individual Catholics, rather than the history of large congregations.

The aim of this book is to identify the sources needed to trace Catholic family and local history in England and Wales. We begin by outlining the history and structure of English Catholicism, placing it in context. Sources are scattered in a wide range of record offices and libraries, so Chapter 3 offers a guide to locating records, and to conducting research. Early Catholic history has to be studied through the records of its enemies, the state and the established church, so

Chapter 4 deals with the various records created as a result of the penal laws. There follow chapters on records of Catholic baptisms, marriages and burials, Catholic clergy and religious, and a variety of other sources of information.

Abbreviations used in the text

Gandy (1) Gandy, M. *Catholic family history: a bibliography of general sources*. Michael Gandy, 1996.

Gandy (2) Gandy, M. *Catholic family history: a bibliography of local sources*. Michael Gandy, 1996.

Gandy (3) Gandy, M. *Catholic Missions and Registers*. 6 vols + atlas vol. Michael Gandy, 1993.

Chapter 1

POST-REFORMATION ROMAN CATHOLICISM, 1558–1828

Between the sixteenth and the nineteenth century, Roman Catholics were feared in England in much the same way that Communists were feared in the twentieth century, and as Muslims are feared today. The fear was greatly exaggerated. But antagonism was deeply rooted in historical events, and in very effective Protestant propaganda. The horrors of 'Bloody Mary' were described in graphic detail in John Foxe's *Book of Martyrs*[1], which was perhaps the most successful piece of propaganda in British history. The rising of the Northern Earls in 1569, the Ridolfi Plot of 1571, the Throckmorton Plot of 1583, the Parry Plot of 1584, the Babington Conspiracy of 1586, the Bye Plot of 1603, and the Gunpowder Plot of 1605 all associated Roman Catholicism with treason. The Spanish Armada seemed to demonstrate the lengths to which Roman Catholics were prepared to go in order to destroy English Protestantism. Anti-Papalism gradually became deeply embedded in the English psyche, and supposed Roman Catholic hostility to England was heartily reciprocated.

Yet when Elizabeth came to the throne in 1558, the country she ruled had been deeply Catholic. She was faced with the colossal task of transforming the Catholic priesthood into a Protestant ministry. The many reversals of official religious policy in the previous two decades, and the consequent shortage of clergy, did not help. The Catholic priesthood had merely sustained the faith. The Protestants undertook the much more difficult task of conversion.

The success of Protestantism hung in the balance for most, if not all, of Elizabeth's reign. It depended upon the mechanism of enforcement, which was very weak. Attendance at prayer book services became a legal

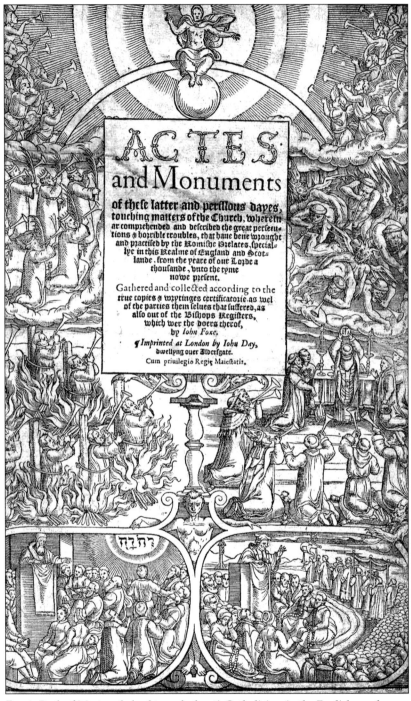

Foxe's Book of Martyrs helped to embed anti-Catholicism in the English psyche.

obligation, theoretically enforced by the threat of a one shilling fine for each absence. Churchwardens were expected to enforce attendance, but many were themselves crypto-Catholics. Enforcement did, perhaps, become easier when the Crown was increasingly threatened by risings, plots, and invasion.

The old religion was a complex of social practices, many of which were retained. Conservative clergy made their prayer book services as much like masses as they could; some conducted both public Protestant services and secret Catholic masses. The Reformation confused many laity, who simply continued the tradition of attending their parish church, despite the 'stripping of the altars'[2] and the many changes in the liturgy imposed by the Protestant regime.

Elizabeth I, excommunicated in 1570.

They 'did not well discern any great fault, novelty or difference from the former religion, that was Catholick, in this new sett up by Queen Elizabeth, save only the change of language'. 'Unawares to themselves, [they] became neutrals in religion'.[3] A new tradition was being created.

In the early decades of Elizabeth's reign, the Roman Catholic hierarchy made minimal effort to support English Catholics.[4] They assumed that there would soon be a Roman Catholic succession; all that was required was to wait. It was a reasonable assumption; Elizabeth nearly died of smallpox in 1562. Her most likely heir at that time was Mary Queen of Scots – a Catholic. And it was true that most would have happily reverted to the old ways had Elizabeth reigned no longer than her sister.

The Elizabethan bishops perforce had to work with Marian priests, such as Christopher Trychay, the conservative incumbent of Morebath (Devon), who had probably been implicated in the 1549 Prayer Book rebellion.[5] The hierarchy distrusted such old priests. But they had too few genuinely Protestant priests to replace them. Trychay managed to keep his benefice until he died, sixteen years after Elizabeth's accession. He was a devoted pastor, reluctant to desert his flock by speaking out. Those of his compatriots who were more outspoken – or perhaps less lucky – suffered deprivation.

Mary Queen of Scots.

It is probable that many deprived priests nevertheless continued their ministrations. At least, the government assumed they were doing so. As early as 1563, Lord Keeper Bacon complained that the common people seldom attended church.[6]. The Bishop of Worcester complained about 'Popish and perverse priests which misliking [Protestant] religion have forsaken the ministry and yet live in corners, are kept in gentlemen's houses and have great estimation with the people where they marvellously pervert the simple and blaspheme the truth'.[7] In the 1560s, over 150 Marian priests were active in Yorkshire, and another seventy-five in Lancashire.[8]

Meanwhile, the Oxford dons who fled to the Continent in 1558 had one aim in view: the restoration of the ecclesiastical establishment as it had been before 1558. Many continued their academic careers at Louvain and elsewhere on the Continent. Others served in the continental church; Owen Lewis, for example, had been a fellow of New College Oxford; he was consecrated as Bishop of Cassano, in the Kingdom of Naples, in 1588.[9] For most of the 1558 exiles, correctness of doctrine was what mattered. They merely waited for the restoration of the hierarchy, seeing no need for mission, or to make provision for successors to the Marian clergy.

In England itself, there was minimal direction from the hierarchy. Many Catholics continued to worship in parish churches, the great majority insisting on their loyalty to the Queen. Elizabeth herself was disinclined to 'make windows into men's souls'. Her government rarely sought to inflict the full legal penalties for recusancy (that is, the refusal to attend church services).[10] Indeed, some of the officials responsible for enforcing the law against Papists were themselves sympathetic towards them. Furthermore, recusant owners of advowsons were able to continue presenting their own nominees to Church of England livings until 1605. Thereafter, the universities were supposed to exercise these rights of patronage, although there were instances where Catholics continued to make presentations.

Lay Catholics owed loyalty to the Crown as well as to the Pope. Considerations of conscience could lead to conformity as well as to recusancy. Worshippers were emotionally involved with their parish church. Their ancestors were buried there. Catholics' approach to participation in church services varied. Some used subterfuge. Mathew Haigh, a Yorkshire yeoman, for example, was accused of 'unreverent receiving'. It was said that 'when he should have receiued the communion, the bread being given him, did not eat it, but conveyed it into his book, and likewise did not drink ye wine, as himselfe hath synce reported, but onely toke it into his mouth'.[11] Others simply refused to take communion, which many saw as a mockery of the mass – the Cornish rebels of 1549 had called it a 'Christmas game'. Many, however, were prepared to attend matins, the normal Sunday morning service, ignoring the Pope's 1566 ban on attending heretical services, but not unduly compromising their beliefs. Initially, the Catholic hierarchy permitted occasional conformity under certain conditions.

Compromisers, sympathetic conformists and church papists gave considerable strength to the Catholic community throughout the penal years, especially in the early decades of Elizabeth's reign. Conversely, although anti-recusant laws were in place, mere recusancy was not systematically persecuted by the government in the first decade of Elizabeth's reign. Consequently, records are few.

It was not until the 1570s that Roman Catholics realised that their church in England needed to become a missionary church in order to survive. William Allen even had to defend the abandonment of clerical dress by priests in England. Nevertheless, his success in founding a college to train the priests who would be needed when the hierarchy was restored set the future direction of English Roman Catholicism. Allen did not, however, anticipate that Douai would become a missionary centre. He merely created the mechanism for training English priests. It was his recruits who saw the need for missionary priests who could take the Roman interpretation of the gospel to Protestant England.

Many joined the Society of Jesus, which had been founded by Ignatius of Loyola as an evangelistic and disciplined order earlier in the century. Loyola's 'spiritual exercises' were brought to Douai. In 1574, Allen despatched a few seminarists to England. Douai did not have room for all those students who sought admission, so a string of overflow colleges were founded – Valladolid, Madrid and St Omer. In 1579, an English College under the direction of Jesuits was founded in Rome, and the following year Allen persuaded Everard Mercurian, the Superior of the Jesuits, to found a Jesuit Mission to England. The first missioners were Edmund Campion, Robert Persons[12] and Ralph Emerson.

The aim of the seminarists was to reconcile schismatics, and to lead church papists into recusancy. Conversion was seen as important in the long term, but unrealistic. The priority was the preservation of the Catholic community in the face of immense dangers. Priests ordained abroad committed treason merely by stepping on English soil. Campion was executed within a year of landing, and Persons had to flee back to the Continent. Cuthbert Mayne had already been hung, drawn and quartered in 1577 – the first of many seminary priests to suffer for their faith. When William Weston arrived in England in 1584, there was not a single Jesuit at liberty in the country. In 1586, he too was arrested and imprisoned at Wisbech Castle.

When priests from Douai began to arrive in England, and especially when Jesuits arrived in 1580, Catholic compromisers began to find themselves under serious attack. Jesuits brought with them a much stricter understanding of the boundary between conformity and recusancy. They argued against acceptance of Anglican ministrations, seeking to 'reconcile' church papist 'schismatics' to the Catholic church.

Many Marian priests responded to the Jesuits with fear and suspicion; they were regarded as meddlesome innovators, likely to provoke persecution. The Jesuits retaliated by accusing Marian priests

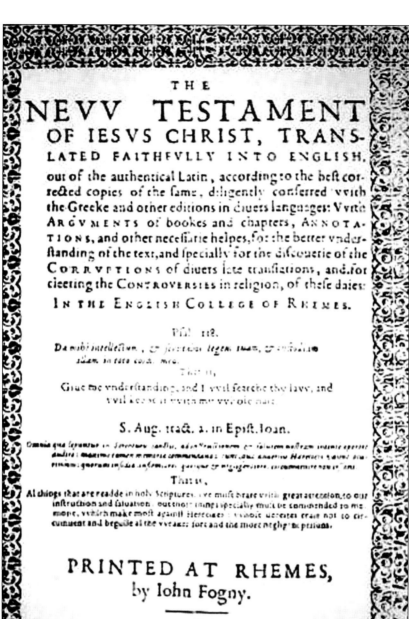

THE
NEVV TESTAMENT
OF IESVS CHRIST, TRANS-
LATED FAITHFVLLY INTO ENGLISH,

out of the authentical Latin, according to the best cor-
rected copies of the same, diligently conferred vvith
the Greeke and other editions in diuers languages: Vvith
ARGVMENTS of bookes and chapters, ANNOTA-
TIONS, and other necessarie helpes, for the better vnderstanding of the text, and specially for the discouerie of the
CORRVPTIONS of diuers late translations, and for
cleering the CONTROVERSIES in religion, of these daies:

IN THE ENGLISH COLLEGE OF RHEMES.

Psal. 118.

Da mihi intellectum, & scrutabor legem tuam, & custodiam
illam in toto corde meo.

Giue me vnderstanding, and I vvil searche thy lavv, and
vvil keepe it vvith my vvhole hart.

S. Aug. tract. 2. in Epist. Ioan.

Omnia quæ leguntur in Scripturis sanctis, ad instructionem & salutem nostram intente oportet
audire: maxime tamen in memoria commendanda: quæ aduersus Hæreticos valent plu-
rimum: quorum insidiæ infirmiores quosque & negligentiores, circumuenire non cessant.

All things that are readde in holy Scriptures, vve must heare vvith great attention, to our
instruction and saluation: but those things specially must be commended to me-
morie, vvhich make most against Heretikes: vvhose deceites cease not to cir-
cumuent and beguile all the vveaker sort and the more negligent persons.

PRINTED AT RHEMES,
by Iohn Fogny.

1582.

CVM PRIVILEGIO.

The seminarists undertook a Catholic translation of the Bible. The Douai-Rheims New Testament was published in 1582.

of spineless conformity and spiritual inadequacy. Thus began the dispute between Jesuits and the seculars which rumbled on for centuries, as we will see.

Recusancy began with non-communicating. This was followed by refusal to attend church. Finally, Roman Catholic priests able to conduct baptisms and marriages were sought. By 1583, reconciliations were

Guy Fawkes and the other conspirators alarmed whilst digging their mine.

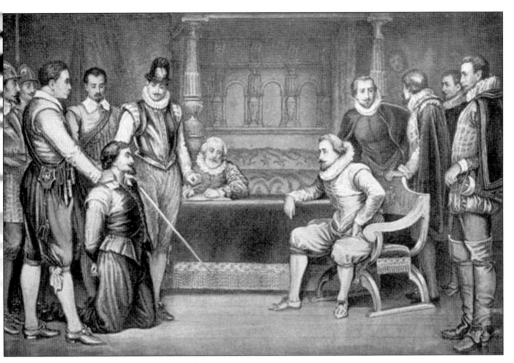

James I interrogates Guy Fawkes.

being made on a considerable scale. Conversions, however, were few.

Many of the reconciled followed the lead of their social superiors. When manorial lords compromised or converted, their tenants frequently followed. In terms of influence, Catholicism was seigneurial. In the late sixteenth century, 45.6% of Norfolk Catholics who came to the notice of the authorities were gentry.[13] But the authorities were only interested in the gentry; the names of the many yeomen, husbandmen, labourers, and tradesmen who followed their lead were not as frequently recorded.

The advent of the seminarists marked the end of mutual compromise between the government and English Catholics that had lasted for over a decade. The 1569 Northern Rising caused the government serious concern over the loyalty of Catholics. In the following year, the Papal Bull, *Regnans in Excelsis*,[14] pronounced Elizabeth excommunicate and required Catholics to withdraw their allegiance. Recusant prosecutions began to be ramped up. In Winchester Diocese, the diocesan act book records a mere 303 prosecutions of Catholics between 1561 and 1569. In 1570, there were 245 prosecutions, mostly in the last few months after the Bull had been published. Those prosecuted included many gentry. They also included forty-three churchwardens – the very ones who were supposed to enforce attendance at church.

Prosecution did not, however, remain constant thereafter. It was not the government's preferred option. Rather, there were spates of prosecutions consequent on events such as the Armada and the Gunpowder plot. Between 1598 and 1602, Hampshire witnessed numerous prosecutions; there were so many that it was necessary to create a separate book of *Processus contra Recusantes*, which recorded 587 citations.[15] Even so, many Catholics continued to emphasise their loyalty to the Crown. In 1587, as the scale of Spanish preparation for invasion became clear, leading Catholics were vocal in their loyalty to the Crown, and pleaded to be allowed to fight – but instead were incarcerated in the Bishop of Ely's diocesan palace. The government acknowledged their loyalty, but thought incarceration was essential to demonstrate to the Spanish that no support for them would be forthcoming if they invaded.[16]

Recusancy was particularly prevalent among gentlewomen. Protestantism deprived wives of their jurisdiction over a whole range of ritual functions, such as fasting and the keeping of holy days. Single women lost the possibility of entering a religious order. Elizabethan recusancy was driven, to some extent, by the matriarchs of the Catholic community. Unlike their menfolk, they did not have to decide whether it was worth compromising their families' wealth, position, and security for the sake of conscience. In 1604 it was reported that 'many straing persons repair to the house of Mrs Vrsaley Cholmley, which come not to the church and there have bene Seminaryes kept in her house'.[17]

Recusancy did not always depend on the gentry. In some places, religious trends were determined not by them, and not by the official church, but by the standards set by an entire community. People conformed to the mores of the community they lived in, not to mores set by some external power. The fact that there were 120 recusants in Ripon in 1604 was probably due to this type of conformism, rather than to gentry influence: the parish had no gentry capable of exercising such influence.[18]

By the time Elizabeth died, Protestants had established a tradition of their own. The passage of years, combined with the threat of penalties for recusancy, meant, for many, the slow but steady acceptance of the new tradition. By 1603, the number of those who were not prepared to accept the new Protestant tradition was low. It has been estimated that perhaps a mere 40,000 of the English population of 2,500,000 gave their allegiance to Rome.[19] In early seventeenth-century Yorkshire, there were probably only around 3,000 Catholics in a population of around 200,000.[20] A return made in 1604 identified 2,461[21] of their names; they included 622 non-communicants, i.e. church papists.

The great majority of Catholics lived in the North and, to a lesser extent, the Midlands. Only 412 names of Catholics can be identified in Elizabethan Norfolk.[22] In the 1590s, there were perhaps a mere 300 recusants in the whole of the West Country.[23] Numbers were, however, slowly increasing. By 1641, there were perhaps 60,000 Catholics in England and Wales.[24] Everywhere, support was concentrated around the homes of the Catholic gentry and aristocracy – places like Stourton in Wiltshire, whose lord was forced to sell up in 1714 because recusancy cost them so much.

Persecution forced some compromises. Catholics were supposed to attend mass regularly, but there were too few priests for that to be possible. It was essential to find other methods of sustaining the faith. Consequently, some priests encouraged the development of practices which enabled the faithful to achieve a direct personal relationship with the divine, without priestly mediation. When medieval mystics had indulged in such practices, they had frequently been viewed with suspicion. Now, they were seen as important means of sustaining the faith. Catholics had to focus on the functions of their religion, rather than strict adherence to institutional forms.[25]

Persecution also made it difficult to organise and give direction to the mission. The last Marian bishop died in 1585. Cardinal Allen died in 1594. There was no one apart from the Pope himself who could claim any sort of general authority over English Catholics. The vacuum was filled to some extent by the Jesuits, led from 1586 until his execution in 1606 by Henry Garnet. He met all Jesuit missioners once or twice a year, and exercised limited control over secular clergy. He had a particular care for newcomers from the seminaries, and maintained them in London until they had a definite place to go. The seculars, however, had little say in the overall direction of the Mission; Garnet took the decisions personally.

The seculars were not entirely happy with that situation (although some were sympathetic to the Jesuits). Division developed between secular and Jesuit, between conservatives hankering after canonical hierarchy, and Jesuits who believed that the future of English Catholicism depended on disciplined missionary priests. Those divisions were stirred up by the disputes over the whole question of leadership and authority in the English Mission which became known as the Wisbech Stirs.[26]

Wisbech Castle served as an internment centre for Catholics during Elizabeth's latter years. By the 1590s, over thirty Catholics were imprisoned there.[27] The majority – mainly Jesuits – wanted a regulated communal life. Some seculars did not, and objected to the way in which Jesuits tried to impose their discipline. Wider issues were also involved. Jesuits were seen as stirring up plots against the Crown, which rebounded on all Catholics; the seculars denied that the Pope had any right to exercise political influence in England. Similar disputes broke out at the English College in Rome between 1594 and 1598; many students left to join the Benedictine order.

The seculars hoped that the restoration of the canonical hierarchy would diminish Jesuitical power, and enable the church to take back control of patronage from the gentry. The appointment of an archpriest in 1598 was intended to meet some of their arguments. However, their hopes were disappointed. George Blackwell, the new archpriest, was close to the Jesuits. And although he had authority over secular priests, he had none over either the religious orders, or gentry patrons. He was not a bishop. Blackwell's appointment was opposed by many of the seculars, who became known as the appellants.

The desire of the seculars for a bishop was partially met in 1623, with the appointment of William Bishop as Vicar Apostolic. Bishop was consecrated as Bishop of Chalcedon, but the full diocesan hierarchy was not restored, and he lacked the canonical powers of a diocesan bishop.

In the early seventeenth century, the Jesuits thrived. Their numbers rose from eighteen in 1598 to forty in 1606. By 1623 there were 120, enough to justify the creation of a separate English Province of the society. In 1639, just before the outbreak of the Civil War, there were 193.

The Benedictines also reappeared in England under the early Stuarts. Just one English Benedictine survived in 1603. Sigebert Buckley became a monk at Westminster Abbey after it was refounded by Queen Mary, but was imprisoned at Wisbech Castle. In 1607, he was persuaded to admit new members to the English Congregation, in order to preserve its continuity.

Benedictines were contemplatives. In the opinion of Augustine Baker, the very idea of going into England would be a 'miserable distraction' to monastic life.[28] The early seminarists had not expected them to be involved in the English mission. Nevertheless, some seminary students did find Benedictinism attractive, and monasticism proved to be the point on which conservative opinion coalesced in defence of tradition and against the Jesuits.

The Benedictine revival that took place after 1600 was not, however, quite what the conservatives had in mind. The Spanish Benedictinism encountered by students was activist and modernistic in character, not far removed from the Jesuit ideal. Baker's attitude was actually out of the mainstream of contemporary Benedictinism, although the contemplative life continued to hold attractions for some.

Disputes within the church did not change the realities of life on the English mission. Nor did the appointment of archpriests, or, indeed, Vicars Apostolic. In the early days of the Mission, most priests were peripatetic, travelling by horse or foot from house to house, although usually with a base. The priest would arrive at a house late in the afternoon, spend the evening hearing confessions, giving spiritual direction, saying mass and preaching, then riding on to the next house in the morning. He was likely to use subterfuge, changing his name, changing clothes, and changing his route regularly. He depended on Catholic gentry to give him shelter. Many had 'priest holes' constructed in order to offer hiding places (see p.183–4). Such hiding places sometimes placed the gentry themselves in great danger. In Tudor and Stuart times 'every attempt to count Catholics reveals them as coagulated in local groups at the centre of which a gentleman's household will usually be found'.[29]

Therein lay the rub. Gentry support came with a price. Gentry who sheltered priests expected them to provide first for their own families. Priests were expected to act as private chaplains, to tutor their hosts' children, and perhaps to serve as stewards on their hosts' estates. Gentlemen wished to appoint their own priests, not to have priests imposed upon them by the hierarchy. The idea of an itinerant priest who would serve all the Catholics in the area allotted to him was not always acceptable to them. Proselytising Protestants was seen by the gentry as suicidal, and not something they allowed their priests to attempt.

Despite these restrictions, priests increasingly settled in gentry houses. It gave them a permanent home.[30] By 1625, whatever the priests thought, Catholic gentry reigned supreme over the mission, and continued to do so for 150 years. That supremacy, however, was never unquestioned. Many examples of non-seigneurial recusant communities in Elizabethan Norfolk have been identified.[31] There are many seventeenth-century examples of independent mission stations supported by the yeomanry and based in public houses or inns.[32]

The persecution of Catholic priests gradually faded in the eighteenth century. A few were imprisoned as a result of an act of 1700, and the Franciscan Paul Atkinson languished in Hurst Castle from 1700 to 1729. Priests continued to be imprisoned occasionally in the early years of George III's reign. However, in 1769 Lord Mansfield gave it as his opinion that evidence of ordination was required for a successful prosecution of a Catholic priest. No subsequent prosecution succeeded.

The decline of persecution contributed to the fact that priests began to reassert their independence of the gentry in the late eighteenth century. It was not, however, until the restoration of the hierarchy in 1850 that clerical dominance became fully established.

The strength of Catholicism cannot be measured by the number of recusants alone. Aveling has argued that 'the astonishing allegiance to Catholicism of so many compromisers, conformists and church-papists or even nominal protestants, seems a more striking evidence for the strength of English Catholicism than the straightforward heroic recusancy of the relatively few.[33] All the Stuart kings had Catholic wives. Charles II himself is said to have declared his allegiance to Rome on his death-bed. Catholic gentry had a great deal of influence at Court under the Stuarts. Many church papists held crown offices. For example, William Drury was the master of the Prerogative Court of Canterbury. There was even a Catholic receiver of recusancy fines![34] Yet recusants were legally excluded from public office. That exclusion, admittedly, had the advantage that Catholics were saved the trouble of serving on juries or as Justices of the Peace, and were able to avoid the heavy expenditure occasioned by serving as sheriffs or standing for Parliament.

In the early seventeenth century, Rome considered an episcopal presence in England inopportune: it would create problems for the

Church. Indeed, any public advocacy of Roman Catholicism did that. Politicians opposed to Catholicism had the upper hand; this was clearly demonstrated in 1641, when the strength of Puritanism in Parliament resulted in the execution of eleven Catholic priests.[35] Catholics were not keen on fighting during the Civil War itself; many considered neutralism to be the best option. Those who did fight mostly fought for the King, and consequently suffered at the hands of Parliamentary sequestrators.[36] Of course, after the Restoration of Charles II they benefited from royal sympathy and an easing of repression.

Despite Charles's sympathy, the false 'revelations' of Titus Oates in 1678 demonstrated how easy it remained to stir up anti-Catholic feeling. The accusations made by Oates marked the (temporary) return

Titus Oates in the pillory.

James II, the last Roman Catholic king of England.

of persecution, imprisonment for many, execution for some and confiscation of much Jesuit property. One hundred priests were arrested, seventeen were executed, twenty-three died in prison and eleven Catholic peers were imprisoned for treason. Oliver Plunket, Archbishop of Armagh, was the last Catholic priest to die for his faith in England. And Catholic Peers were excluded from the House of Lords.

The situation changed dramatically – but briefly – when the Roman Catholic James II ascended the throne in 1685. The Pope, sensibly, remained cautious. He almost immediately appointed John Leyburn as Vicar Apostolic, an office which had been effectively vacant since Richard Smith fled England in 1632. But it was not until 1688 that the country was divided into four districts, each with its own episcopal Vicar Apostolic. Even then, the new office-holders could not exercise ordinary episcopal jurisdiction, or upset the status quo.

James himself, however, was incautious and anxious to start the process of converting England. He was too hasty. His actions led to widespread opposition. He lost the support of most Lords Lieutenant. Some Protestant Justices of the Peace refused to work with the Catholics he appointed to the bench. The birth of an heir precipitated the invasion of William of Orange and James's flight into exile.

English Catholics celebrated some conversions, but gained little from James's short reign. Half of the Catholic peerage fled with James. Michael Ellis, who had just been appointed as a Vicar Apostolic and placed in charge of the Western District with a salary of £100 per year, and a grant of £500 from the Royal Exchequer, was imprisoned in Newgate Gaol and deported. He was not replaced as Vicar Apostolic until 1713.

James's deposition was not, however, catastrophic for the Catholic cause. Some penal legislation was enacted in the ensuing century. However, prosecutions continued to be sporadic and infrequent – although admittedly Catholics suffered after the Jacobite Rebellions of 1715 and 1745, and during the Gordon Riots of 1780. The rebellions actually received little support from Catholics, except in Lancashire.[37]

Following the 1688 Revolution, the policy of fining recusants was abolished. Rather, when the new land tax was introduced in 1692, recusants were required to pay double. There were also attempts to make them incapable of inheriting or purchasing land, but in practice these had little impact. Catholic lawyers could easily devise trusts and settlements which evaded restrictions on land ownership.[38]

After the 1715 Jacobite rebellion,[39] Catholics were held to be collectively guilty of rebellion (despite the lack of involvement of the majority), and were required to register their estates. When the Atterbury Plot of 1723 again drew attention to their potential for disaffection, the information registered was used to subject them to another tax – although it was many years before it was fully collected.[40]

Catholics again played little role in the 1745 rebellion. Although chapels were looted at the time, the government took steps to restrain the mob. In the following decades, the penal laws gradually fell into desuetude. The Anglican ecclesiastical authorities continued to identify recusants, but did little more than that. High Anglican priests who hated the Toleration Act for permitting the growth of nonconformity showed increasing tolerance to Catholics. It was left to the Anglican Society for the Propagation of the Gospel to promote legislation strengthening the penal laws. But even they thought it necessary to do so 'without persecution and violence'.[41]

Priests were increasingly able to live openly. They were addressed as 'Mr' and dressed as laymen, except during mass. Their dependence on gentry and aristocracy gradually decreased as independent missions were founded. Many Catholics, both lay and clergy, left money to fund them.[42] By 1725, Newcastle, Hexham, Gateshead, Durham, Sunderland, Darlington and Stockton all had at least one priest living independently within their boundaries.[43] By the mid-eighteenth century, public chapels were replacing the houses of gentlemen as the bases of Catholic clergy. The presence of a chapel at Bath was even mentioned in a popular 1753 guide for visitors, despite the fact that Catholic chapels remained illegal until the Catholic Relief Act 1791. Unfortunately, it was not sufficiently inconspicuous. It was destroyed in the Gordon riots of 1780.

Surviving Catholic gentry families were thriving, despite – or perhaps because – their numbers were falling. Many families lacked male heirs, sometimes because their sons had become religious or were priests. Surviving families sometimes augmented their wealth by marrying the heiresses of those which died out. In 1767, when a census of Catholics was taken, a mere sixty-seven gentry households with a resident squire, his family, five or more servants and a priest were counted.[44]

The number of Catholic peers was also falling. By 1791, there were only seven. Since 1714, eight peerages had become extinct, and there had been nine apostacies.[45] In Staffordshire there were only three Catholic gentry families left in the 1770s.[46] The gentry were ceasing to dominate the church.

Persecution, as has been seen, gradually ceased to be government policy. Rather, it became mob activity. The Catholic Relief Act 1778 abolished the oath that prevented Catholics becoming army officers, ended the prosecution of Catholic priests and schoolmasters, and

Bath Roman Catholics now worship at St John's.

removed the ban on Catholic purchase and inheritance of land. It did not, however, prevent anti-Catholic rioting. Populist opposition led to the Gordon Riots of 1780. The London mob gutted several chapels and

The Gordon Riots, painted by John Seymour Lucas.

looted Catholic homes. In the provinces, the Western Vicariate's archives in Bath were destroyed.

Populist prejudice continued for at least another century. Whenever legislation favourable to Catholics was proposed, there were riots, frequently aimed particularly against the Irish.[47]

A much more extensive Catholic Relief Act was passed in 1791. Catholics were again required to take an oath of loyalty, but its wording was not offensive to their religion. Those who took it ceased to be liable to prosecution. The Act ended the registration of Catholic estates and wills, opened the legal profession to Catholics and required Catholic places of worship to be registered. It did not, however, end double land tax, or allow Catholics to hold public office.

This Act coincided with the beginnings of the French Revolution, and a flood of French Catholic refugees. By 1797, refugee numbers totalled 5,500 priests and 5,950 laity.[48] The refugee influx was accompanied by the return to England of the numerous schools, seminaries, and monastic establishments which had operated on the Continent during the penal period. The expulsion of religious English from France and the lands conquered by Napoleon led to the establishment of a number of schools, seminaries and monasteries in England, including Downside, Ampleforth, Stonyhurst, Oscott and Ushaw.

Roman Catholicism was expanding.[49] Catholicism was growing as rapidly as Methodism, and for similar reasons. The growth of the latter was due to itinerant proselytisers. Roman Catholics practised catechising rather than proselytising. That paid off. We have no reliable sources for estimating numbers, but it is clear that there was considerable expansion. The Compton census has been used to estimate that there were 11,500 Catholics in 1676, although this number has been characterised as 'tentative and incomplete'.[50] The census of 1767 recorded 66,690 Catholics: a considerable increase in almost a century. A few years later, in 1773, the Vicars Apostolic put the numbers at 59,000.[51] Between 1760 and 1850, the number of Catholics increased ten-fold.[52] The Industrial Revolution began the transformation; this was followed by the Irish deluge, commencing in around 1790. Priests trained in repatriated seminaries such as Oscott and Downside were able to put their training to good effect without restraint in the new industrial towns. This was the golden age of the mission.

Between 1760 and 1850, the social make-up of the community dramatically changed. The Church expanded into the new industrial areas of the West Riding, south-east Lancashire, the East Midlands, and South Wales. In the regions of its traditional strength, such as other parts of Lancashire, the North-East and the Midlands, Catholics were moving from rural areas into industrial towns. A 1767 survey shows that agricultural labourers and domestic workers who were in full-time employment were heavily outnumbered by industrial workers and handicraftsmen. They were on the move; a study of fifteen Catholic congregations in Staffordshire reveals that none of them had a majority of members who had resided in the same place for more than ten years. Mid-nineteenth-century Catholicism was heavily concentrated in northern industrial towns.

Irish immigration had always been present, but it did not become important until the late eighteenth century. Even in Liverpool, the Irish only constituted 20% of the baptisms that took place in 1783.[53] Irish immigration only began to increase dramatically in the final decade of the eighteenth century. Overall, it accounted for perhaps 70% of the expansion of the community that took place between 1770 and 1850.

By 1840, there were 80,000 Catholics in Liverpool. In 1845, even more Irish flooded in as the Great Famine struck. By 1850, 80% of Catholics nationwide were Irish and working class.[54]

English Catholics became a minority in the church – but a very substantial minority, and their numbers expanded too. In most cities, congregations were formed from a minority of relatively wealthy English Catholics and a majority of poor Irish. Social geography, however, meant that some congregations remained aristocratic in tone, while others catered solely for poor Irishmen. Former embassy chapels in London's West End catered for the aristocracy and professional people. New chapels built in Wapping, Bermondsey and Southwark between 1770 and 1800 catered for immigrants, probably mainly Irish.

The Industrial Revolution ended gentry dominance of the Roman Catholic church. We have already noted the fall in their numbers. The gentry could not even continue their dominance of the rural church. Many congregated in London or Bath, deserting their rural estates. Some counties had few or no resident Catholic gentry in 1800.

Meanwhile, urban missions were flourishing. There were two congregations in Birmingham with over 2,000 members.[55] Restraint could no longer be imposed on the clergy; they had an audience which was ready to listen. The inconspicuous reserve which circumstances required of the gentry-dominated church in the early eighteenth century had no appeal whatsoever to rebellious and destitute Irishmen. One commentator noted that:

> in manufacturing districts there is found a greater spirit of enquiry and a greater freedom of thought and expression, than in the less populous parts of the country, and consequently the pastor who avails himself of this opportunity is sure to find his zeal rewarded with many conversions and an abundant harvest of souls.[56]

For Catholics, the church was a worldwide community centred in Rome. In contrast to both Anglicans and dissenters, they were constantly exposed to overseas influence, helped by the fact that before around 1800 all their priests were educated abroad.

The story of English Catholicism in the nineteenth century is dominated by Catholic emancipation, Irish immigration, and the restoration of the hierarchy in 1850. In 1800, all that hampered the church was the lack of priests, and the destruction of continental seminaries during the French Revolution. The Revolution helped change English attitudes; Roman Catholicism began to be seen as a bulwark against the anti-religious atheism which seemed to be sweeping the Continent.

The question of political emancipation was placed firmly on the agenda by the 1800 Act of Union with Ireland, but not finally settled until the Catholic Emancipation Act 1829. It was the result of a long campaign, but the immediate trigger was the election of Daniel O'Connell as MP for Co. Clare. As a Catholic, he was unable to take

Daniel O'Connell.

the necessary oaths, but denial of his right to serve outraged opinion in Ireland. Faced with the potential of serious rebellion, Parliament abolished restrictions on Catholics holding most public offices.

The 1829 Act marked the beginnings of a dramatic and unexpected change in the character of Catholicism. The denomination entered the mainstream of English religious activity. Priests trained at Oscott and Ushaw were, for the first time, free to practise their vocations in their own ways, without the restraint imposed upon them by either the penal laws or the gentry. The Oxford Movement in the Church of England had an important impact, although those who followed Newman in 1845 and converted to Rome were relatively few in number, despite the publicity they attracted. The majority of new Catholics were Irish immigrants fleeing the Great Famine.

Irish Catholicism was quite different in character to the English variety. It was still closely intertwined with holy wells, shrines and folk religion. Objects such as crucifixes and holy water were still assigned supernatural virtues.[57] And the Irish were poor. Service to the poor provided the church with much of its appeal to the Irish. Priests established numerous societies and facilities to assist the poor, and to compete with Anglicans and Nonconformists.

As we have seen, the number of Catholics multiplied tenfold in the century before 1850. In 1770, there were perhaps 80,000.[58] By 1850, there were 700,000.[59] The 1851 religious census recorded 252,783 attendees at mass on 30 March 1851.[60] There were only 186,111 seats for them: churches were overcrowded. The difference between 1770 and 1850 was dramatic, but it did take place against the background of rapid growth among evangelical Protestants. Unlike the evangelicals, however, Catholic growth was due primarily to the suffering of Ireland – although it should be noted that the number of recorded attendees at mass in 1851 was actually less than the number of Irish recorded in the census.[61] Irish apostasy was a serious problem for the Catholic church; it has been suggested that perhaps only 30 per cent to 50 per cent of the Irish were practising Catholics.[62]

The Irish invasion meant that the old Catholics were swamped. Nevertheless, the 15th Duke of Norfolk was still widely regarded as the lay leader of English Catholics when he died in 1917. He was probably the wealthiest English Catholic, but a few other landed families also continued to nurture the faith on their estates. The Blundells, the

Cardinal Newman.

Throckmortons, the Scropes, the Tichbornes – names well known in the Catholic world for generations – were still supportive of the Catholic community even in the 1920s. But they sent their offspring to the *Venerabile*, the English College at Rome – and consequently ceded any remaining gentry leadership to the hierarchy. When English students returned from Rome, they brought with them the confidence, authoritarianism, and spiritual energy of Ultramontanism. They had a strong commitment to the conversion of England, and inspired a renaissance which made Catholicism the most successful non-Anglican denomination in the early twentieth century. They also made the English church more Roman than Rome, sought to 'liberate' the church from lay patronage, and enabled the restored hierarchy to pick up the mantle of leadership from the gentry. In an age of uncertainty, authoritarianism appealed.

The huge increase in numbers necessitated administrative change. In 1840, the number of Vicariates Apostolic was increased from four to eight. But the most important change had to wait until 1850, when Pope Pius IX reconstituted the English hierarchy. The metropolitan see was established at Westminster, with twelve suffragan sees. The move met with considerable political opposition in England; however, when the furore had died down, the new Archbishop, Cardinal Wiseman, observed that 'we have not been dragged before tribunals', and that the spirit of the age accepted liberty of conscience.[63]

The monarchical powers of bishops over their clergy were greatly increased. The clergy themselves, however, were not restored to the same position in their parishes. Until the revision of canon law in 1918, priests remained merely assistants in missions under the direct control of the hierarchy. Ideally (and increasingly), the bishop owned the buildings, appointed the priests, authorised their payment, and required regular reports on their activities.

By the nineteenth century, the clergy had become the dominant power in the English church. The title 'Father' began to be adopted for Roman Catholic priests from around 1850. Priests were respected not because of their social status, but because they lived in 'holy poverty', and because of their sacred functions. They were frequently held in deep affection, since they lived in close proximity to their flocks; it was the priest who visited the sufferer from cholera, who stopped fights when the police were afraid to intervene, who fought for the education of Catholic children. Their close relationships with their congregations enabled them to exercise tight control over their activities.

Lay Catholics tended to accept the doctrines taught to them by their priests without question. The church was regarded as the depository of

The North-West Entrance to Westminster Cathedral.

divine truth, and priests were the guardians of that truth. The doctrine of Papal infallibility was defined by the first Vatican Council in 1870. Individual judgement was not acceptable when it diverged from the 'truth' taught by the church. Consequently, Catholicism sought to eject liberal and 'modernist' thought from its midst.

The laity needed to be protected against such ideas. It also needed protection against the perils of nineteenth-century living. That meant education, and, in particular, the education of the Catholic. They needed to be taught how to live as Catholics. If the church failed to teach its adherents, they would be lost to other denominations – or to none. As the *Rambler* put it, 'without the Catholic education of the Catholic poor, all our other efforts are something very like a mockery and a self-delusion'.[64] A huge amount of effort went into the provision of Catholic elementary education. In 1851 there were ninety-nine Catholic schools with an attendance of 7,769 pupils. By 1874, there were 1,484 schools with 100,372 pupils.[65] New elementary schools were regarded as much

27

more important than new churches, despite the pressing need for the latter. Indeed, many schoolrooms were occupied by congregations on Sundays. The concentration on Catholic education transformed the late nineteenth-century church.[66] It also, incidentally, completely reversed Catholic attitudes towards government. During the penal years, Catholics had endeavoured not to draw attention to themselves; now, their indigence led them to vocally demand equal treatment with other denominations in the allocation of state grants for education.

The growth in the number of Catholic schools was accompanied by a steady increase in the number of church buildings, financed by the pennies of the Irish poor. Churches cost much money to run, and even more to build, and there were few able to make substantial contributions. Debts were frequently huge. Diocesan archives tell us more about fundraising than any other subject. Revenue was raised by house-to-house collection, conducted by the priest himself. Despite the poverty, however, where there had been about 560 English churches in 1851, with seats for around 183,000 people, by 1900 there were 1,529. Numbers increased from about 700,000 to over 1,500,000. The growth continued into the twentieth century. In the 1930s there were around 12,000 converts per year, many, admittedly, the product of mixed marriages. In 2010, it was estimated that there were almost 4,000,000 Roman Catholics in England and Wales. There are currently about 3,300 churches, with 875,000 seats.[67] The number of priests has similarly expanded. In 1880, there were 1,946 priests in England and Wales. By 1920 there were almost 4,000, serving over 2,000,000 Catholics, and 400,000 children were in Catholic schools.[68] During the 1940s, the number of priests in England and Wales rose dramatically, by over 1,000; in 1950, there were 6,643.[69]

There was also considerable growth among the religious orders. The task of running schools and building up Catholic communities could not be left to seculars alone, and bishops were keen to encourage growth. The number of priests in religious orders increased from 275 in 1850 to 2,360 in 1950.[70] The number of nuns also increased dramatically; many convents opened girls' boarding schools.

In 1911, the growth in numbers resulted in the division of England into three separate provinces, with Archbishops for Birmingham and Liverpool as well as Westminster. Wales became a separate province in 1916.

The twentieth century saw a steady improvement in the standard of living in the Catholic community. By 1950, the majority of Catholics had ceased to be poor members of the working class. Catholic ranks in northern industrial centres had thinned and dispersed southwards. The typical Catholic was no longer a labourer, but rather a middle-class bank clerk or civil servant with a responsible job.

Twentieth-century expansion took place against the background of steady decline among Nonconformist denominations. Roman Catholicism also posed an increasing challenge to the Church of England as the dominant English church. From the time of the Irish immigration, the Roman Catholic church had been the church of the poor. Unlike the other denominations, there was no question of membership raising you in the social scale. Most priests were drawn from the poorer sections of the community, and the church provided 'a sort of spiritual solidarity of the poor'.[71] That may be why, by the middle of the twentieth century, old prejudices against the church had virtually disappeared, except in Northern Ireland.

The post-war settlement resulted in considerable numbers of Eastern European Catholics settling in Britain. In 1950, there were over 100,000 Poles in Britain, including ninety-two priests. There were also many new immigrants from Ireland. By 1961, 9.7 per cent of marriages were conducted in Roman Catholic churches. Whereas in the 1920s there had been one Roman Catholic wedding for every ten Anglican ones, by the 1960s the proportion was one to four.[72] Between 1959 and 1964, no fewer than 15 per cent of babies born in Britain were baptised by Roman Catholic priests.[73]. Thereafter, however, numbers began to fall. In 1976, the numbers baptised were barely more than half the number baptised only twelve years before. The number of new converts also slumped: 12,000 per year had been the figure in the early 1960s; in 1972, there were fewer than 4,000.[74]

The trend was roughly in line with that experienced by other denominations. It may have been affected by the Second Vatican Council, which challenged clerical dominance and authoritarian attitudes, and replaced the Latin liturgy. For some, it seemed to remove the old certainties. The church's previous success had depended to some extent on those certainties. But the impact of Vatican II on the fall in numbers is a topic of considerable controversy.

FURTHER READING

Numerous works on the history of English Catholicism are available. The aim here is to list a few of the basic modern works which provide useful introductions. Many more are listed by Gandy (1 & 2). A short but sound introduction, together with some documents, is provided in:

• Dures, Alan. *English Catholicism 1558-1742: continuity and change*. Seminar Studies in History. Longman, 1983.

For the whole period from the Reformation until the twenty-first century, see

• Hattersley, Roy. *The Catholics: the church and its people in Britain and Ireland from the Reformation until the present day*. Chatto & Windus, 2017.

The authoritative history of the English Roman Catholic community prior to 1850 is:

• Bossy, John. *The English Catholic Community, 1570-1850*. Darton Longman & Todd, 1975.

Bossy argues strongly that there was little continuity between Marian Catholicism and the Catholicism brought by the seminary priests in the later years of Elizabeth's reign. This has been challenged by:

• Haigh, Christopher. 'The Continuity of Catholicism in the English Revolution', in Haigh, Christopher, ed. *The English Reformation Revised*. Cambridge University Press, 1977, p.176-208.

See also:

• Aveling, J.C.H. *The Handle and the Axe: the Catholic recusants in England from Reformation to Emancipation*. Blond & Briggs, 1978.
• Norman, Edward. *Roman Catholicism in England from the Elizabethan Settlement to the Second Vatican Council*. Oxford University Press, 1986.

A much older work, including numerous documents and much biographical information, is provided by:

- Dodd, Charles. *Dodd's church history of England, from the Commencement of the Sixteenth Century to the Revolution in 1688*, [ed]. M.A. Tierney. [Rev. ed.] 8 vols. Charles Dolman, 1838-43.

For particular periods, see:

- Trimble, William Raleigh. *The Catholic laity in Elizabethan England 1558- 1603*. Belknap Press of Harvard University Press, 1964.
- Walsham, Alexandra. *Catholic Reformation in Protestant Britain*. Ashgate 2014. Collection of essays on the Catholic response to the Reformation.
- Walsham, Alexandra. *Church Papists: Catholicism, Conformity, and Confessional Polemic in Early Modern England*. Boydell Press, 1993.
- Newton, Diana. *Papists, Protestants and Puritans, 1559-1714*. Cambridge University Press, 1998. A basic introduction to the place of Catholicism in English religion.
- McClain, Lisa. *Lest we be Damned: Practical Innovation and Lived Experience among Catholics in Protestant England, 1559-1642*. Routledge, 2004. A fascinating insight into how Catholics lived in penal times.
- Havran, Martin J. *The Catholics in Caroline England*. Stanford University Press, 1962.
- Glickman, Gabriel. *The English Catholic Community, 1688-1745: Politics, Culture and Ideology*. Boydell & Brewer, 2009.
- Turnham, Margaret H. *Catholic faith and practice in England, 1779-1992: the role of Revivalism and Renewal*. Boydell Press, 2015.
- Norman, Edward. *The English Catholic Church in the Nineteenth Century*. Oxford University Press, 1984.

There are numerous works on special topics such as the Wisbech Stirs, Gunpowder Plot and Jacobitism. The following texts offer introductions to some of these topics:

- Law, Thomas Graves, ed. *The Archpriest Controversy: Documents relating to the dissensions of the Roman Catholic clergy 1597-1602 ...*

from the Petyt manuscripts of the Inner Temple. Camden Society New series 56 & 58. 1896-8.

- Fraser, Antonia. *The Gunpowder Plot: Terror and Faith in 1605.* Weidenfeld & Nicolson, 1996.
- Kenyon, John. *The Popish Plot.* William Heinemann, 1972.
- Monod, Paul Kléber. *Jacobitism and the English People 1688-1788.* Cambridge University Press, 1989.
- Haywood, Ian, & Seed, John, eds. *The Gordon riots: politics, culture and insurrection in late eighteenth-century Britain.* Cambridge University Press, 2012.
- Fielding, Stephen. *Class and ethnicity: Irish Catholics in England, 1880-1939.* Open University Press, 1993.

A useful regional bibliography on Irish Catholics is provided by:

- Aspinwall, Bernard. *Arrival, Assertion, and Acclimatisation, or, Context and Contrasts: a Preliminary Checklist of Works on the Irish Catholic Experience in the North West of England.* North West Catholic History Society, 1996.

Many local histories are listed by Gandy (2). A handful of the best can be mentioned here:

- Wark, K.R. *Elizabethan Recusancy in Cheshire.* Chetham Society 3rd series 19. 1971.
- Haigh, Christopher. *Reformation and resistance in Tudor Lancashire.* Cambridge University Press, 1975
- Williams, J. Anthony, ed. *Post Reformation Catholicism in Bath.* 2 vols. Catholic Record Society, 65-6. 1975-6
- Williams, J.Anthony. *Catholic Recusancy in Wiltshire 1660-1791.* Monograph series 1. Catholic Record Society, 1968,
- Aveling, Hugh. *Post Reformation Catholicism in East Yorkshire, 1558-1790.* East Yorkshire Local History Society, 1960.
- Aveling, Hugh. *Northern Catholics: the Catholic Recusants of the North Riding of Yorkshire, 1558-1790.* Geoffrey Chapman, 1966.
- Aveling, J.C.H. *Catholic Recusancy in the City of York, 1558-1791.* Monograph series 2. Catholic Record Society, 1970.

Many English Catholics sought refuge on the Continent. In the nineteenth century, many settled in colonies such as Australia and North America. English Catholics were also active in missions to the indigenous peoples of the British Empire, especially in Africa and Asia. Their movements, and especially emigration to the British Empire, are traced in:

• Davies, John. *The British Catholic Diaspora: A Handbook*. North West Catholic History Society, 2008. This includes brief chronologies and useful bibliographic information.

Chapter 2

THE STRUCTURE OF THE ROMAN CATHOLIC CHURCH

Roman Catholics in sixteenth and seventeenth century England sought to restore the church hierarchy which, in their view, had been destroyed at the Reformation. The church depended on priests; only priests could celebrate the mass, the central rite of the church. Priests were of two kinds: the religious (although not all religious were priests), and the secular. The religious were members of religious orders: Jesuits, Benedictines, Franciscans, Dominicans. The Jesuits dominated in England, at least in the early seventeenth century. Relations between seculars and religious were not always good. Some missions showed a marked preference for priests from a particular order. Bath, for example, was a Benedictine stronghold.[1]

After the Reformation, Roman Catholic priests continued to be celibate (unlike their Anglican counterparts), but they had no parishes to be responsible for, nor did they have bishops able to support them. Instead they had mission stations from which they frequently had to cover huge areas by themselves. They grumbled that the gentry usurped the role of bishops by choosing their own priests, when canon law required that priests should be under the rule of bishops. The condition of the secular priests was described as 'simple anarchy' in the 1660s.[2]

The problem was, how was the hierarchy going to be restored? On that, there were conflicting and bitter arguments, which have already been discussed. Hierarchy could only be restored by the Pope, but Popes thought restoration inexpedient during the penal era. It was not until 1850, after emancipation had taken place, that the country was divided into dioceses and diocesan bishops and archbishops were appointed.

Catholicism in pre-emancipation England was not the canonical construct that Catholics on the Continent experienced. There were no Roman Catholic bishops, and no courts to impose discipline. On the Continent mass was normally said in parish churches, not in private houses. In England, the opposite was true. For lower class Catholics, regularity of sacramental observance was impossible. Confirmation was rare. When William Bishop became the first Vicar Apostolic in 1624, he held the first confirmation services for decades.

During the early years, each county was under the authority of a senior priest. It was his responsibility to organise a network of stations. Yorkshire, for example, was divided into a series of circuits, made up of a number of manor and farm-houses where the occupants wished to receive the ministrations of a Catholic priest. There would be perhaps two priests itinerating around each circuit. They resided somewhere central to their circuit, but remote from other places, and travelled incognito. The practice of residing in gentlemen's houses became normal by around 1600.[3]

Prior to around 1750, the Catholic chapel was almost always private, frequently inside a gentleman's house.[4] The church as such could not own property. The authorities would have regarded such property as being dedicated to 'superstitious uses', and therefore liable to seizure. However, in the mid-eighteenth century, as risk diminished, chapels on the ground floors of country houses, where estate tenants and workers could easily gain access, became common. When the Stourton family sold their manor in 1714 they erected and retained a new chapel at Bonham, to serve the surrounding area. Such chapels became increasingly common as the century progressed. In the nineteenth century, many Anglican converts established their own private chapels. Some of these remained private, but others developed into important churches. Elsewhere, rooms were frequently hired for services. Many missions held their services in school rooms, but increasingly new churches and presbyteries were built in urban areas.

A variety of temporary expedients were devised to deal with the problem of governance. From 1598 to 1621, government was in the hands of an archpriest. As has been seen, he was replaced by a Vicar Apostolic (although there was frequently no office holder). In 1688, four vicariates were created, each with a Vicar Apostolic. The Vicars were bishops in name, but lacked the powers of a diocesan bishop. Instead, they were

The nineteenth-century interior of Bonham Chapel.

responsible directly to the *Congregatio de Propaganda Fide* in Rome.

The first Vicar Apostolic founded a Chapter for secular priests, although he had no canonical authority to do so. It helped to govern the church for centuries, although its authority was not recognised by Rome.[5] In 1850, on the restoration of the hierarchy, it was held to have been illegal from the outset.[6] Throughout the penal era, the whole structure of ecclesiastical governance in England was regarded by many as uncanonical and unsatisfactory.

In 1840, the number of Vicars Apostolic was doubled. The restoration of the hierarchy followed in 1850. Initially, thirteen dioceses were created, with the see of Westminster as their Archdiocese. Bishops, canons, and rural deans were appointed.

Gentry control of church property, and of the payment of priests, was steadily whittled away. From 1850, the hierarchy expected that the laity would not play any role in church governance. Cardinal Wiseman's attitude was encapsulated in his remark that 'We will call you [the laity] forth when the Church of God needs your aid'.[7] At grass roots level, however, there was little change. It was not until the twentieth century that parish priests regained their full canonical status. The 1850 restoration of the hierarchy was not accompanied by the restoration of the parish, with its own priest, and with its administrative independence. There were no parish councils, and even where lay committees existed for the purpose of fundraising, the bishops sought to bring them under their control.[8] The bishops considered that parishes, with their rights and special interests, would hinder rapid expansion of the church. The parish, it was argued

> is a territorial division of the Church founded to provide for the religious needs of a Catholic population already existing. A mission is a territorial division of the Church founded to create a Catholic population and thus prepare the way for further missions and finally for true parishes of their nature stable.[9]

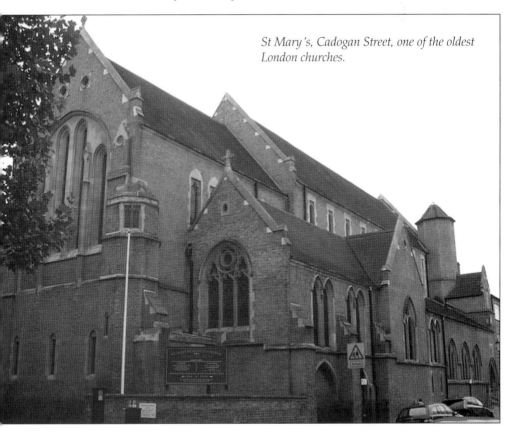

St Mary's, Cadogan Street, one of the oldest London churches.

The Church at Sheerness, with its presbytery.

The restoration of the parish in the English church had to wait until 1918, when a new code of canon law was adopted. By then, as has been seen, there had been a massive expansion of the church, and it was ready for a more settled polity at the local level. 1911 also saw the rearrangement of the church into three separate provinces: Westminster, Birmingham and Liverpool. More have since been added. For a map of modern dioceses, visit **www.r-c.org.uk**.

For researchers, another important event was the 1983 promulgation of a revised code of canon law. It required an archive repository in every Catholic diocese. Every diocese now has one. Their importance will be outlined in Chapter 3.

FURTHER READING

For the early Vicars Apostolic, see:

- Hemphill, Basil. *The early Vicars Apostolic of England, 1685-1750.* Burns & Oates, 1954.

For the Old Chapter prior to 1706, see:

• Sergeant, John. *An account of the Chapter erected by William, Titular Bishop of Chalcedon, and Ordinary of England and Scotland*, rev. William Turnbull. James Darling, 1853.

Many of the Chapter records are held by Westminster Diocesan Archives. A list of priests in 1692 found among them is printed in:

• Stanfield, Raymund, ed. 'Particulars of priests in England and Wales, 1692, from the archives of the Old Brotherhood', *Miscellanea 7*. Catholic Record Society, 9. 1911, p. 103-114.

Another list of priests from the same source is printed in:

• Stanfield, Raymund, ed. 'Obituaries of Secular priests 1722-1783, from the Archives of the Old Brotherhood, formerly the Old Chapter of England', in *Obituaries*. Catholic Record Society 23. 1913, p.1-15.

An earlier necrology (listing of deceased members) of the Chapter is included in:

• Guiney, Louise F. 'A Chapter necrology, Oct. 1670 – Feb. 1678', *Miscellanea 3*. Catholic Record Society 3. 1906, p.98-104.

The administrative structure of the church after the restoration of the hierarchy in 1850 is discussed by:

• Sweeney, Morgan V. 'Diocesan Organisation and Administration', in Beck, George Andrew, ed. *The English Catholics 1850-1950*. Burns Oates, 1950, p.116-50.

Chapter 3

PRELIMINARIES TO RESEARCH

This book is concerned primarily with using a variety of records to trace the history of Roman Catholics in England and Wales since the sixteenth century, and identifying specific individuals. Genealogists are likely to concentrate on the records of baptisms, marriages and burials (discussed in Chapter 5), but their family history is likely to be much augmented by other sources. Records of fines, forfeitures, imprisonments and executions suffered by Catholics were kept by the persecutors. Spiritual events such as conversions, reconciliations and first communions, as well as the careers of the clergy, were recorded by the church. There are a wide variety of other sources which help us to identify individual Catholics in time and place, and provide valuable information on local communities.

There have, admittedly, been many losses of records over the centuries, but the problems caused may frequently be remedied by the survival of duplicate records elsewhere. Thus the recusant rolls in the National Archives class E 377 are duplicated in E 376. And the fines and forfeitures recorded in them should also be recorded in Quarter Sessions records, found in county record offices.

This book assumes that you are already familiar with research methods in genealogical research, with more general family and local history sources, such as census records, the civil registers, wills and trade directories, with the institutions that hold these sources, and with the genealogical internet. These will be touched upon only in so far as they may throw light on Catholic history. Those who have not undertaken research before may find it useful to consult:

• Wintrip, John. *Tracing your pre-Victorian ancestors: a guide to research methods for family historians.* Pen & Sword, 2017.

The outstanding guide to genealogical sources, despite its age, is still:

- Herber, Mark. *Ancestral trails: the complete guide to British genealogy and family history.* 2nd ed. Sutton Publishing, 2004.

The most up-to-date general guide to the internet is:

- Paton, Chris. *Tracing Your Family History on the Internet: a Guide for Family Historians.* (2nd ed. Pen & Sword, 2014).

For a useful dictionary, see:

- Few, Janet. *The Family Historian's Enquire Within.* 6th ed. Family History Partnership, 2014.

Record offices, libraries and the internet are the prime workshops of family and local historians. It is important to know which of these are likely to be most useful, what information they can provide, and how they should be used. All record offices hold a wide range of private family and estate papers, which may include the correspondence and papers of Roman Catholic clergy and laymen. For a detailed listing of over 400 record offices in the United Kingdom, visit:

- Find an archive in the UK and beyond
  http://discovery.nationalarchives.gov.uk/find-an-archive

Most record office websites include a catalogue of their archival holdings, although these are rarely complete. There are also a number of union catalogues. Again, these are far from complete, but they may record information not available on institutions' own websites. See

- The National Archives Discovery Catalogue
  http://discovery.nationalarchives.gov.uk
- Archives Hub
  www.archiveshub.ac.uk
  For archives held by universities and colleges.

- AIM 25
  www.aim25.ac.uk
  For the London area
- Archives Wales
  www.archivesnetworkwales.info

Many Roman Catholic records are held in specialist institutions associated with the church. Such institutions also frequently hold many printed books. A number of these institutions are listed in

- ABTAPL Theological and Religious Studies Collection Directory
  www.newman.ac.uk/abtapl/database/contents.html

Roman Catholic records tend to be more dispersed than those of other denominations, and it is therefore doubly important that you should be aware of the wide range of libraries and record offices holding such records. Institutions such as the National Archives, local studies libraries and county record offices are important resources for all researchers. In addition, the Catholic researcher needs to be aware of diocesan archives, and of various other Catholic institutions which hold important collections.

There are two previous guides to Catholic sources which are still worth consultation, although both are now rather dated:

- Pollen, John Hungerford. *Sources for the History of Roman Catholics in England, Ireland and Scotland from the Reformation period to the Emancipation, 1558-1795.* Helps for Students of History 39. Society for Promoting Christian Knowledge, 1921.
- Steel, D.J. *Sources for Roman Catholic and Jewish Genealogy and Family History.* National Index of Parish Registers 3. Phillimore, for the Society of Genealogists, 1974

A. RECORD OFFICES

Record offices are warehouses for archives. Indeed, they are sometimes referred to as archives, but the word is probably better kept to refer to the contents of record offices. Archives provide almost all the written evidence we need to trace our ancestors. Without them, most genealogical books could not have been written, and the internet would be of little use to genealogists.

Catholic registers of baptisms, marriages and burials, with other parish records, are likely to be held either in the local record office, or in diocesan archives. More recent registers are held by the relevant church. For the deposit policy adopted by most dioceses, see Gandy (3). Many other records relating to Roman Catholics are held by local and national record offices. However, canon law requires diocesan archives to be retained in the church's own repositories (which may also hold parish records). Roman Catholic diocesan records are rarely found in local authority record offices. Diocesan archive repositories are listed below (p.47–56).

The National Archives

The records of central government in the National Archives include a huge amount of information relating to the persecution of Roman Catholics. The trials of priests, the fining of recusants, and governmental

The National Archives. The records of government persecution of Catholics will be found here.

policy towards the faith are all well documented. This documentation will be discussed in Chapter 4. It can be searched at **http://discovery. nationalarchives.gov.uk**. Note that the majority of documents are not fully indexed in this catalogue; frequently documents of several hundred pages are described in just a few lines of text. The researcher must be prepared to identify documents that are potentially relevant merely from that description. Hopefully, the information in the rest of this book will assist in that task.

For a discussion of relevant records at the National Archives, see:

• National Archives: How to Look for Records of Catholics
www.nationalarchives.gov.uk/help-with-your-research/ research-guides/catholics

Parliamentary Archives
The Parliamentary Archives, of which the House of Lords Record Office is now a part, hold a few official collections relevant to Roman Catholicism. For example, a number of censuses of Roman Catholics were conducted on the orders of the House of Lords, which now holds the returns to them. These will be discussed in Chapter 4. For current information on the Archives, visit:

• Parliamentary Archives
www.parliament.uk/business/publications/parliamentary- archives

A basic introduction to the Archives is provided by:

• Bond, Maurice. *The Records of Parliament: a guide for genealogists and local historians.* Phillimore & Co., 1964.

For a more detailed guide, see:

• Bond, Maurice F. *Guide to the Records of Parliament.* HMSO, 1971.

British Library
The British Library probably holds all the books and periodicals mentioned here. Your need to consult them, however, is unlikely to gain

you access to this library, since most are readily available in many other libraries. Access to the British Library is generally only granted when the information you require cannot easily be found elsewhere.

That condition for entry will be met if you need to consult any of the library's vast collection of manuscripts. The library's online manuscripts' catalogue records over 2,000 entries for documents relating to Roman Catholics. A handful of these are mentioned in later chapters. The catalogue, and much other information, is available at:

- The British Library
  www.bl.uk

In addition to the online catalogue, there are also many printed catalogues. For a helpful guide to these, see:

- Nickson, M.A.E. *The British Library: guide to the catalogues and indexes of the Department of Manuscripts.* 3rd ed. British Library, 1998.

Bodleian Library, Oxford University

This library has important collections such as those collected by Rawlinson, Tanner and Clarendon. These include, for example, lists of London Papists in 1714, and of recusants in several counties, temp George I.[1] The collections of a few statesmen are discussed in Chapter 11. A guide to the collections is provided by:

- Bodleian Libraries Manuscripts and Rare Books
  www.bodleian.ox.ac.uk/subjects-and-libraries/collections/ manuscripts

For a printed catalogue, see:

- Madan, Falconer, et al, eds. *A summary catalogue of western manuscripts in the Bodleian Library at Oxford which have not hitherto been catalogued in the Quarto series* (7 vols. in 8 [vol. II in 2 parts], Oxford, 1895-1953. This is also available at **http://libguides.bodleian.ox.ac.uk/medieval-sc/summary**

National Library of Wales

The National Library of Wales **www.llgc.org.uk** holds the records of the Court of Great Sessions (the Welsh Assize courts), and the Anglican Church of Wales. Both these collections record the persecution of recusants. The papers of a number of Catholic families are also held. For a detailed discussion, see:

• Huws, Daniel. 'Catholic Records in the National Library of Wales', *Catholic Archives* 14, 1994, p.65-70.

Local Record Offices

There are numerous local record offices. County record offices were originally created to house the records of Quarter Sessions. They frequently also hold Church of England diocesan records. Diocesan and Quarter Sessions records are important for Catholic history, since they record extensive attempts to suppress Catholicism. Local record offices frequently also hold the papers of local Catholic families. Less frequently, they may hold mission registers. Lancashire Record Office, for example, holds examples of just about every type of record mentioned in this book. Admittedly, Lancashire was one of the most Catholic counties in England, but its holdings typify the range of Catholic archives that can be held in similar record offices. See:

• Foley, B.C. 'Lancashire Record Office and Roman Catholic Records', *Catholic Archives* 7, 1987, p.28-38.

Roman Catholic Official Records

The official records of Roman Catholic Vicariates, and, subsequently, dioceses, are generally stored in their own private archives; they are rarely to be found in local record offices. Twentieth-century parish records (and sometimes older documents) are frequently still held by parishes, and initial inquiries should be directed to the relevant priest. Catholic diocesan repositories usually hold episcopal correspondence, visitation papers, accounts, educational records and files relating to the priests, parishes, and religious houses in the diocese. There are likely to be mission and parish records such as mission registers, parish newsletters and notice books, and building plans. Runs of diocesan magazines and Catholic directories, together with other journals, are frequently held. There may also be antiquarian collections, sometimes including many transcripts of documents held in Rome and other places.

Roman canon law specifies the classes of records that are to be retained by diocesan repositories. The journal *Catholic Archives* includes many brief descriptions of their holdings. Most back issues have been digitised at **https://catholicarchivesociety.org/the-journal-of-the-catholic-archives-society's**. For a union catalogue, which is only small at the moment, but likely to grow, see:

- Catholic Heritage: Network of Archives and Libraries of the Catholic Church
  www.catholic-heritage.net

Diocesan record offices are frequently run by volunteer staff. It is important to appreciate that these are private archives, and that they may be unable to deal with inquiries from genealogists – although local historians may receive a warmer welcome. For a full list of Catholic record offices, visit:

- Religious Archives Group: Roman Catholic Church
  https://religiousarchivesgroup.org.uk/advice/directory/christianity/catholic
- Catholic Archives Society: Archives Directory
  https://catholicarchivesociety.org/archives-directory

See also:

- Williams, Margaret Harcourt. 'Catholic archives and family history', *Catholic Ancestor* 13(1), 2010, p.20-28.

Diocesan Record Offices
All Catholic dioceses have their own repositories. These are listed below. Information about them can usually be found on their websites, in the journal *Catholic Archives* and in other publications. However, there appears to be little published information regarding the archives of the dioceses of Hallam and Menevia.

Arundel Cathedral.

ARUNDEL AND BRIGHTON
- Jackson, Sandre. 'Archival Holdings of the Diocese of Arundel and Brighton', *Catholic Archives* 19, 1999, p.42-6.
- Diocese of Arundel and Brighton: Diocesan Archives
  www.dabnet.org
  Search 'Archives'.

BIRMINGHAM
The Archdiocese of Birmingham Archives holds the archives of the Midland District (1688–1840), the Central District (1840–1850), the Diocese of Birmingham (1850–1911) and the Archdiocese of Birmingham (1911–present). In addition to the usual material, they include the papers of eighteenth-century Vicars Apostolic, and Dodd's collection of material for a biographical dictionary of English Catholics, among much else. Other collections include, for example, the archives of St Mary's College, Oscott, and Sedgley Park School. There are also many Catholic parish records. See:

48

- Archdiocese of Birmingham Archives
  www.birminghamarchdiocesanarchives.org.uk/index.asp
- Sharp, John. 'Birmingham Archdiocesan Archives', *Catholic Archives* 22, 2002, p.6-9.
- McEvilly, J.Dennis. 'Birmingham Diocesan Archives' *Catholic Archives* 1, 1981, p.26-31.

BRENTWOOD
The Diocese of Brentwood was founded in 1917, so most of its archives are twentieth-century. They are described in:

- Foster Stewart. 'Brentwood Diocesan Archives', *Catholic Archives* 15, 1995, p.20-24.
- Diocese of Brentwood: Archives
  www.dioceseofbrentwood.net/diocese/archives

CARDIFF
Few Cardiff archives date from earlier than around 1900. They are listed by:

- Chidgey, Dan. 'The Archives of the Archdiocese of Cardiff', *Catholic Archives* 26, 2006, p.37-41.
- Archdiocese of Cardiff 1916-2016: Administration of the Archdiocese of Cardiff
  http://rcadc.org/administration

CLIFTON
The archives of the Western Vicars Apostolic, and of the Diocese, were deposited for a time at Bristol Record Office, but are now held by Clifton Diocese Archives Department. Early archives of the Western District were destroyed during the Gordon Riots in 1780. The core of the remaining archive is provided by episcopal correspondence dating from around 1770. See:

- Harding, J.A. 'The Archives of the Diocese of Clifton', *Catholic Archives* 11, 1991, p.3-10.
- Bradley, Anne. 'Interim report on Clifton Diocesan Archives deposited at Bristol Record Office', *South Western Catholic History* 4, 1986, p.6-11.

- Clifton Diocese Archives Department
  **www.cliftondiocese.com/departments/services-commissions/
  archives-department**

EAST ANGLIA
The archives of the Cathedral of St John the Baptist, Norwich, plus some old parish records, are deposited with the Diocesan archives. See:

- Cowton, Dora. 'Diocese of East Anglia: Summary List of Archives',
  Catholic Archives 25, 2005, p.11-14.

HEXHAM AND NEWCASTLE
This repository holds some of the records of the Northern Vicars Apostolic (dating back to the seventeenth century), as well as the archives of the Diocese, of St Mary's Cathedral, Newcastle, and of a number of Catholic organizations. Parish registers are generally deposited in local record offices. See:

- Gard, Robin. 'The Archives of the Diocese of Hexham and
  Newcastle', *Catholic Archives* 19, 1999, p.24-41.
- Diocese of Hexham and Newcastle: Archives
  www.rcdhn.org.uk/about_the_diocese/looking_up_records.php

LANCASTER
The diocese was founded in 1924. The only published information on archival holdings is provided by:

- Diocese of Lancaster: Bishops' Archives
  www.lancasterdiocese.org.uk/our-bishop/bishops-archives

LEEDS
Leeds diocesan collections include the archives of the former Diocese of Beverley, and of the Northern District Vicars Apostolic – although many archives of the latter can also be found in the Ushaw collection at Durham University, and, to a lesser extent, at Lancashire Record Office. The papers at Leeds consist mainly of the personal papers of the bishops since 1688. See:

- Archives: Diocese of Leeds
  www.dioceseofleeds.org.uk/archives
- Bradley, George T. 'Leeds Diocesan Archives', *Catholic Archives* 2, 1982, p.46-51.

LIVERPOOL

This repository holds bishops' papers 1840–1996, many volumes of newspaper cuttings, and the twentieth-century records of the Union of Catholic Mothers, among much else. For Archdiocesan archives, together with those of Liverpool Cathedral, see:

- Metropolitan Cathedral of Christ the King, Liverpool: Archives
  www.liverpoolmetrocathedral.org.uk/history-heritage/ cathedral-diocesan-archives

Liverpool Metropolitan Cathedral.

The late twentieth-century papers of Archbishop Worlock, together with other archives, are described in:

• Whittle, Meg. 'Liverpool Archdiocesan Archives', *Catholic Archives* 19, 1999, p.18-23.

Early parish registers have been deposited in Lancashire Record Office and in Liverpool City Record Office.

MIDDLESBROUGH

This diocese was formed in 1878 by sub-dividing the Diocese of Beverley. Many parish registers are held in the archives; indeed, the bulk of the diocesan archives relate to parishes. They are described in:

• Smallwood, David. 'The Middlesbrough Diocesan Archives' *Catholic Archives,* 26, 2006, p.49-55.
• Middlesbrough Diocese: Archives
  http://middlesbrough-diocese.org.uk/about/archives

NORTHAMPTON

Some records of the Eastern District since 1840 have been preserved at Northampton Diocesan Archives. There are also a few parish registers, and much other material relating to parishes. That is in addition to the records of the diocese itself. See:

• Osborne, Margaret. 'The Northampton Diocesan Archives', *Catholic Archives* 21, 2001, p.41-4.
• Diocese of Northampton: Administration and Consultative Bodies
  www.northamptondiocese.org/THEDIOCESE/DIOCESAN DEPARTMENTS/AdministrativeandConsultative/tabid/77/ Default.aspx

NOTTINGHAM

Archives dating from 1851 include correspondence and reports, files on particular parishes, religious houses, priests and students, and some parish records. See:

• Dolan, Anthony. 'Nottingham Diocesan Archives', *Catholic Archives* 3, 1983, p.9-19.

See also:

• Diocese of Nottingham: Archives & History
www.nottingham-diocese.org.uk/12_Archives/archive_home. html
Includes indexes to a collection of parish magazines dating from 1869, and to the Diocesan yearbook since 1921.

PLYMOUTH
The majority of Plymouth Diocesan archives consist of files for individual parishes. There are also the pastoral letters of early bishops, and the answers of priests to a historical survey carried out by Bishop Vaughan in 1872. Little survives prior to 1850. For a detailed discussion, see:

• Smith, Christopher. 'The Archives of the Plymouth Diocese',
Catholic Archives 10, 1990, p.17-20 & 39.
• Diocese of Plymouth: Diocesan Archives
www.plymouth-diocese.org.uk/index.php/curia-agencies-and-commissions/commisions/diocesan-archives

PORTSMOUTH
• Portsmouth Catholic Diocese: Diocesan Archives
www.portsmouthdiocese.org.uk/directory/organisation/768.htm

SALFORD
The Diocese was founded in 1851, but little survives from the nineteenth century.

• Diocese of Salford: Diocesan Archives
www.salforddiocese.net/archives
• Lannon, David. 'Salford Diocesan Archives', Catholic Archives 16, 1996, p.8-10.

SHREWSBURY
Shrewsbury Diocesan archives date back to 1851; they include the bishops' correspondence, many parish files, financial and educational records, and much else. For full descriptions, see:

- Marmion, John P. 'The Shrewsbury Diocesan Archives', *Catholic Archives* 14, 1994, p.37-43.
- Diocese of Shrewsbury Archives
  www.dioceseofshrewsbury.org/about-us/diocese-of-shrewsbury/archives

SOUTHWARK
Most of Southwark's archives date from the foundation of the diocese in 1850. They are described in:

- Archdiocese of Southwark: Diocesan Archives
  www.rcsouthwark.co.uk/Archives.html
- Clifton, Michael. 'Southwark Diocesan Archives', *Catholic Archives* 4, 1984, p.15-24.

WESTMINSTER
Westminster Diocesan Archives holds what is probably the most important official collection of Catholic archives in the country. Its archives include, according to the website, 'the papers of the bishops, the history of individual parishes and schools, the documents of Catholic societies and the workings of diocesan administration'. They also include much material pre-dating the restoration of the hierarchy, including numerous letters and papers of Cardinal Allen and the Vicars Apostolic, including correspondence with Rome. There are also confirmation lists, a few papers from Douai, records of the 'Old Brotherhood' (see above, p.36 and 39), and some material relating to the Jacobites. The website has a number of useful leaflets on 'Family History'. Visit:

- Westminster Diocesan Archives
  http://rcdowarchives.blogspot.co.uk

A digitised version of the Archives catalogue is available at **discovery. nationalarchives.gov.uk/download/GB0122%20MSS**. See also a lecture by the archivist:

- Schofield, Nicholas. 'The Westminster Diocesan Archives ', *Catholic Archives,* 28, 2008, p.50-56. Also available at
  https://religiousarchivesgroup.files.wordpress.com/2012/03/westminster-diocesan-archive-2007.pdf

Westminster Cathedral.

WREXHAM

• Byrne, Kathryn. The Archives of the Diocese of Wrexham', *Catholic Archives*, 26, 2006, p.42-8.

Other Institutions

For the archives of seminaries, and of religious orders, see chapters 7 and 9. The following notes give details of important Catholic collections held by universities:

DURHAM UNIVERSITY

The University's Special Collections hold the important collections of Ushaw College, which descended from the English College at Douai. In addition to Ushaw's own archives (which include some material from Douai), the collection includes the papers of the English College at Lisbon (see below, p.139–40), and some records of the Northern Vicars Apostolic. The University is now also responsible for the Catholic National Library, which holds numerous transcripts of mission registers made by the Catholic Family History Society. The Library's other holdings are discussed at **www.dur.ac.uk/theology.religion/about/news/?itemno=25936**. For the Ushaw College collection, see:

• Ushaw College
  https://www.dur.ac.uk/library/asc/localother/ushaw.htm

See also:

• Sharratt, M. 'The Ushaw Collection of Manuscripts', *Catholic Archives* 4, 1984, p.4-8 & 14.

LIVERPOOL HOPE UNIVERSITY

The University holds the Gradwell Collection of rare Catholic books, together with a number of similar collections. The archives of Nugent Care, a Catholic charity concerned with child welfare, which ran several childrens' homes, are also held. Visit:

• Liverpool Hope University. Sheppard Worlock Library Special Collections
  www.hope.ac.uk/gateway/library/specialcollections/

OVERSEAS INSTITUTIONS

Continental repositories hold much information on English Catholics, and especially on the European diaspora. The Vatican Archives are particularly important; it has been estimated that perhaps 25,000,000 names are mentioned in them[2]. See:

- Blouin, Francis X., ed. *Vatican Archives: An Inventory and Guide to Historical Documents of the Holy See.* Oxford University Press, 1998.
- Archivum Secretum Vaticanum
  **www.archiviosegretovaticano.va/content/archiviosegretovati
  cano/en.html**

A variety of earlier works are listed by Gandy (1).

Many transcripts from the Vatican Archives, the English College at Rome and other continental archives were made for the Public Record Office in the nineteenth and early twentieth century, and are now in The National Archives, classes PRO 31/9-10. Some of these were published in:

- Rigg, J.M., ed. *Calendar of State Papers Relating To English Affairs in the Vatican Archives … .* 2 vols. HMSO, 1916. Vol. 1, 1558-71. Vol.2. 1572-78. Available online at **www.british-history.ac.uk/search**.

The reports of foreign ambassadors provide much information on English Catholicism. Those sent to Venice are particularly informative, and are calendared in:

- Brown, Rawdon, et al., eds. *Calendar of State Papers Relating To English Affairs in the Archives of Venice, existing in the archives and collections of Venice and in other libraries of Northern Italy.* 38 vols. H.M.S.O., 1864-1947. Covers 1202-1674, but mostly 16-17th c. Online at **www. british-history.ac.uk/search/series/cal-state-papers-venice**

Reports from Spanish ambassadors are calendared in:

- Hume, M.A.S., ed. *Calendar of Letters and State papers relating to English Affairs, preserved principally in the Archives of Simancas.* 4

vols. HMSO, 1892-9. Covers 1558-1603. Online at **www.british-history.ac.uk/search/series/cal-state-papers—simancas**

Spanish archives also contain many documents of interest. For some relevant material, see:

- Loomie, Albert J., ed. *Spain and the Jacobean Catholics*. Catholic Record Society 64 & 68. 1973-78. Vol.1. 1603-1612. Vol.2. 1613-1624.

B. BOOKS AND LIBRARIES

Books are important to family historians. You need to know how to find them, and what they might tell you. In general, books will give you far more detailed and authoritative guidance than websites. There are numerous works dealing specifically with Catholic history. For example, brief biographies of numerous Catholics are contained in biographical dictionaries. There are innumerable transcripts, calendars and indexes of original documents in printed form, not all available on the internet. Many have been published by the Catholic Record Society. In order to identify relevant books, you need to consult library catalogues and bibliographies. The most useful bibliographies for the present purpose are those compiled by Michael Gandy. These are indispensable for the serious researcher into Catholic history:

- Gandy, M. *Catholic family history: a bibliography of general sources.* Michael Gandy, 1996.
- Gandy, M. *Catholic family history: a bibliography of local sources.* Michael Gandy, 1996.

For an update, visit:

- A Booklist for English Catholic Family History in England **https://catholicfhs.wordpress.com/2013/05/16/a-book-list-for-catholic-family-history-in-england/**

Once you have identified the books you need, you can either purchase them, or search catalogues to locate them in libraries. You might find them in a wide variety of different libraries. The catalogues of most public and university libraries are online. There are also a number of union catalogues. See, for example, **http://copac.jisc.ac.uk**.

The catalogue of the Society of Genealogists records over 1,800 items relating to Roman Catholicism. Visit **www.sog.org.uk**. Family Search **https://familysearch.org** provides access to the huge microfilm collections housed in the Latter-Day Saints Family History Library. It also has a substantial number of digitised images of original sources, which are free to access and which rival in size some of the commercial hosts listed below.

Many books (including some mentioned in succeeding chapters) have been digitised and made available on the internet. Huge collections of out-of-print books and journals can be found at (among others):

- Wayback Machine Internet Archive
  https://archive.org
- Hathi Trust Digital Library
  www.hathitrust.org

C. ROMAN CATHOLIC INSTITUTIONS
There are a number of societies devoted to the study of Roman Catholic history in England and Wales since the Reformation. Some of these publish books and journals; others maintain libraries and archives.

Catholic Record Society
The most important publisher is the Catholic Record Society, which has already been mentioned. Many volumes in its record series are mentioned elsewhere in this book. For a full list, visit:

- The Catholic Record Society
  http://catholicrecordsociety.co.uk/

The Society also publishes the major journal in the field:

- *British Catholic History.* Catholic Record Society, 2015- . In its previous incarnations, this was known as *Biographical Studies 1534-1829* (vols. 1-3, 1951-6), and as *Recusant History* (vols. 4-31, 1957-2014).

Catholic Family History Society
Family historians should join the Catholic Family History Society, which can offer much useful advice on research. Its journal, *Catholic Ancestor*

(formerly *ECA Journal*), published three times per year, contains many useful articles, which are listed on its website. It has also published numerous transcripts of original sources. Numerous unpublished transcriptions of original sources made by members are now held by Durham University (see above, p.56), but listed on the society's website. The society is also currently (October 2017) planning the release of the Margaret Higgins Database, which will index 250,000 Catholic names, 1607–1840, found in diverse sources. See:

- Catholic Family History Society
  http://catholicfhs/online

Catholic Archives Society
This society, as its name implies, is primarily for those who have charge of Catholic archives, but its journal, *Catholic Archives* (see above, p.47), occasionally includes descriptions of particular collections, and may be of interest to researchers. Some back issues can be downloaded from its website. The society has published a number of occasional papers and advice leaflets (the latter are also downloadable), primarily of interest to Catholic archivists. Visit:

- Catholic Archives Society
  http://catholicarchivesociety.org/

English Catholic History Association
This association runs a series of visits and lectures on matters of Catholic interest, and issues an online newsletter. The lectures are available online in both print and as podcasts. Visit:

- English Catholic History Association
  https://echa.org.uk/

Regional Societies
There are a number of regional catholic history societies, most of which issue regular journals containing relevant articles. These include:

- East Anglian Catholic History Society
  https://catholiceastanglia2016.wordpress.com
  Established in 2016; its journal is *Orientale Lumen.*

- Essex Recusant Society: Brentwood Diocesan Historical Society
  www.catholic-history.org.uk/sechs/index.html
  The society's journal, formerly known as the *Essex Recusant*, (1959–85) has been published as *South Eastern Catholic History* since 2009. It incorporates the former *London Recusant* (1971–78).
- Isle of Wight Catholic History Society
  http://iow-chs.org/
- Midland Catholic History Society
  https://midlandcatholichistory.org.uk/
  This society brought together separate societies in Staffordshire and Worcestershire. Both societies formerly had their own journals, *Staffordshire Catholic History* (1961–88), and *Worcestershire Recusant* (1963–88). The website includes an index to both of these, and to their continuation, *Midland Catholic History* (1991–).
- North-East Catholic History Society
  www.rcdhn.org.uk/general_directory/diocesan%20_societies/ nechs/nechs.php
  This website includes an index to *Northern Catholic History* (the Society's journal), nos. 1 to 57, 1975–2016.
- North-West Catholic History Society
  www.nwcatholichistory.org.uk/
  This Society's journal is *North West Catholic History* (1969–). Its website includes a digitised version of A.J. Mitchinson's *Catholic family historian's handbook*, which was originally published in 1999. It is now outdated, but may still be useful.
- The Postgate Society and its Origins
  http://middlesbrough-diocese.org.uk/the-postgate-society-and-its-origins
  For Middlesborough Diocese
- Wales and the Marches Catholic History Society
  www.wamchs.btck.co.uk
  The website includes a list of the contents of the Society's journal, *The Old Faith / Yr Hen Ffydd*, together with details of its publications.

Another regional journal was published, not by a society, but by an abbey:

- *South Western Catholic History.* 30 vols. Downside Abbey, 1983-2012.

Chapter 4

ROMAN CATHOLICS UNDER PENALTY AND AFTER EMANCIPATION: GOVERNMENTAL RECORDS

A. THE PENAL LEGISLATION

If the anti-Catholic legislation passed during the reign of Elizabeth I and her successors had been rigorously enforced, the survival of English Catholicism would have been in doubt. This legislation penalised recusancy and the promotion of Catholicism, and imposed various anti-Catholic oaths. At times, these laws were savagely enforced. However, that was not the intention of the authorities. The acts were there to terrify potential offenders, to deter, but not necessarily to be enforced. The government was primarily interested in keeping tabs on the leaders of Catholicism. Consequently, governmental records are likely to mention Catholic gentry much more frequently than the lower classes.

In the early years of Elizabeth's reign, enforcement was lax. However, when the Pope excommunicated Elizabeth in 1570, enforcement temporarily became much more rigorous. The Spanish Armada, the Gunpowder Plot, and the Popish Plot, all had the same effect. The government, however, could also be sympathetic towards Catholicism. We have already seen that Catholics had a great deal of influence at the Stuart Court.

Prosecution could be useful for fiscal purposes. When the Crown needed additional revenue, the punishment of delinquents was encouraged. Charles I in particular relied on recusancy fines during the years of his 'personal rule' without Parliament. Recusants also

The Spanish Armada.

sometimes had to pay double when national levies such as the subsidy and the land tax were imposed.

Most proceedings against Catholics were for recusancy. However, there were many other 'crimes' for which prosecution was possible. Mass attendance, the saying of mass, priest-harbouring, 'Popish' baptism of children, clandestine marriage or burial by Catholic rites, unlicensed teaching, sending children to continental seminaries and possession of Catholic books and devotional objects were all illegal.

When cases came before the Courts, severe sentences were occasionally imposed. But such sentences were intended as exemplary, and provided scope for the Crown to show mercy. Presentments were frequently modified so that offences attracted lesser penalties. For instance, during Charles II's reign, presentments at Wiltshire Quarter Sessions accusing offenders of being absent from church for four weeks were frequently modified to read three weeks, thus reducing the penalty from £20 to a few shillings. The weekly fine was rarely mentioned in these presentments.[1]

Roman Catholics could be prosecuted by both secular and ecclesiastical courts. In general, the ecclesiastical courts were best at detecting the presence of recusants, since they received presentments from churchwardens at local level. However, the aim of ecclesiastical judges was not punishment, but rather the redemption of sinners. The most severe punishment they could impose was excommunication. It was 'a penalty utterly despised by the recusant gentry', according to Bishop Bilson, and had little impact. Secular courts could impose much greater penalties, especially after 1581. Ecclesiastical courts therefore sent on the information they had collected to the secular courts.

Court procedure was slow and bureaucratic. Recusants frequently escaped penalty. They could dodge the apparitor serving the citation to appear. Proceedings in the ecclesiastical courts (and in Quarter Sessions before 1587) could be delayed by not putting in an appearance. They could be strung out in a wide variety of well-practised ways. Prosecutors had to make sure that their cases were watertight. There were many Catholic sympathisers on the bench, and, indeed, a few among Assize judges. In Lancashire, the rector of Wigan, Edward Fleetwood, complained in 1590 that while the Bishop had sent seven hundred names of recusants to the Clerk of the Peace, only about three hundred had actually been indicted, as 'certaine of the Justices of peace' were 'not of the soundest affection'. Furthermore, Judge Walmsley, who sat at the Assizes, himself had a Catholic wife, and had 'made a speech pretending to disbelieve that the country was as full of recusants as the bishop had just told him it was'.[2] The bishops' 1564 report to the Privy Council noted that while over 438 Justices were in favour of the religious changes, 293 were opposed, 125 were neutral, and eighty-five were 'undetermined'.[3]

Lancashire was a hotbed of recusancy. But everywhere it tended to be the minor Catholic gentry who came off worse from the penal legislation. They could ill afford the summonses to court, the legal fees and the tips to apparitors, constables, clerks and other officers. In contrast, the wealthier gentry and aristocracy could obtain letters of protection. They could afford good lawyers, and double subsidies. The costs involved in recusancy were a serious drain for the lesser gentry, who had less influence, and were most likely to find themselves in prison in times of persecution.

The relevant acts can be summarised as follows[4]:

Act of Uniformity, 1559

By this act, everyone was required to attend church[5]. Recusants were to be fined twelve pence for each absence. Attendance at mass, or at any service other than those conducted in accordance with the *Book of Common Prayer*, was forbidden. Fines were to be imposed by churchwardens, and paid into the poor box.[6] Such sums may be recorded in churchwardens' accounts (unfortunately, few of these survive for Elizabeth's reign), although it is likely that they were only infrequently collected. Churchwardens were not always keen on fining their friends and neighbours. Some undoubtedly were Roman Catholics themselves, especially in the early days. There was little check on their enforcement activities.[7]

Act of Supremacy, 1559

All clergy were required to take an oath declaring that the Queen was the supreme governor of the Church of England.

Act for the Assurance of the Queen's Royal Power, 1563

A second refusal of the oath of supremacy was to be deemed treason. The death penalty was to be imposed on any priest saying mass, or any layman procuring it. Those who heard mass were liable for a fine of £66. This act was infrequently enforced.

Act against Papal Bulls, 1571

This act followed the Northern Rebellion of 1569, and the Papal Bull, *Regnans in Excelsis*, which excommunicated Elizabeth. It became high treason to bring Papal Bulls to England, or to absolve or reconcile anyone to the Roman church by virtue of such a Bull. An accompanying act was directed against the landed property of overseas fugitives.

Act to Retain the Queen's Majesty's Subjects in their Lawful Obedience, 1581

A fine of £20 per month was imposed on those who refused to attend their parish church. The offence became indictable at Quarter Sessions as a misdemeanour, although churchwardens continued to be able to levy small fines under the 1559 Act. Failure to pay the £20 made defaulters liable to imprisonment. In practice they were treated as crown debtors, liable to have their assets seized. This act began the practice of treating recusancy as a source of revenue for the Crown. It also increased penalties for saying and hearing mass to 200 and 100 marks[8] respectively, and imposed penalties on Catholic schoolmasters. Those who reconciled converts to the Roman church became liable to capital punishment.

Act against Jesuits and Seminary Priests, 1585

Jesuits and seminary priests were banished from England. It became treason for Englishmen ordained overseas to enter England. Those who sent children to be educated abroad without a licence were to be fined £100.

Act for the More Speedy and Due Execution … of the 1581 Act, 1587

Although Quarter Sessions retained the right to indict recusants, sentences on those convicted could only be imposed at Assizes, at Sessions of Gaol Delivery,[9] or in the Court of King's Bench. Those who failed to appear to answer indictments were to be automatically convicted. Sentencing became the responsibility of Assize judges rather than the potentially more sympathetic Justices of the Peace. This Act clarified the meaning of the 1581 Act by asserting that, on conviction, the fine of £20 per month became payable monthly without further conviction, until the offender submitted. In order to enforce payment, estreats of all convictions made since 1581 had to be delivered into the Exchequer. These estreats form the basis of the recusant rolls (see below, p.85–90). Those who defaulted on the payment of fines ceased to be liable to imprisonment; instead, they forfeited all their goods and two-thirds of their lands.

Act against Papist Recusants, 1593

All persons convicted under previous acts were to be confined to the area five miles around their homes. Copyhold tenements could be forfeited for recusancy. Recusants who had less than 20 marks income per year were required to abjure the realm.

Consolidation Act, 1604
This consolidated previous acts, and made it clear that a convicted recusant who submitted would be excused payment of fines.

Act for the Better Discovering and Repressing of Popish recusants, 1605
This Act was passed in the wake of Gunpowder Plot, and restored jurisdiction over recusants to Quarter Sessions. Presentments listing those who had failed to attend church were to be made monthly by constables and churchwardens. Those convicted under the acts of 1581 and 1587 were required to take communion annually, on pain of a fine of £60. Recusants became liable to a fine of £100 if they approached the Royal Court, practised law or medicine, served as an army or naval officer, or failed to have their children baptised in their parish church. Failure to bury a corpse in the parish graveyard incurred a fine of £20. Recusants could not act as executors or guardians; the husbands of recusant wives were banned from serving in public office.

Oath of Allegiance Extension Act, 1610
The Oath of Allegiance was to be tendered to all Catholics over the age of 18, under penalty of perpetual imprisonment and forfeiture for refusal. Married women recusants could be committed to prison until they took the sacrament, unless husbands paid the penalty of £10 per month. This attacked the common practice of men conforming while their wives remained recusants.

Subsidy Act, 1628
Recusants became liable to double subsidies.

Protestation, 1641
As civil war threatened in 1641, the House of Commons ordered all subjects of the Crown to take an oath (the 'Protestation') declaring their loyalty to the Crown and to Protestantism, and their opposition to 'all Popery and Popish innovations'. This was not strictly an 'act' of Parliament.

Test Act, 1673
All office holders were obliged to take the oath of supremacy and allegiance, to deny transubstantiation, and to receive Anglican communion.

Test Act, 1678
Roman Catholics were excluded from sitting in the House of Lords (they had been excluded from the Commons since 1563).

Land Tax Act, 1692
Double taxation was imposed on recusants liable to land tax.

Act for Further preventing the Growth of Popery, 1700
Recusants became incapable of inheriting or purchasing land. Catholic bishops, priests, and schoolmasters could be subjected to life imprisonment. Informers were offered a £100 reward for information leading to conviction. A similar reward was offered to those who informed on Catholics sending their children overseas to be educated.

Registration of Papists Estates Act, 1715
In the wake of the Jacobite Rebellion, recusants were required to register their estates, in order that they could either be seized or taxed.

Enrolment of Papist Deeds Act, 1716/17
Recusants were obliged to enrol wills and deeds in a court of record.

Catholic Relief Act, 1778
This repealed the Act of 1700, but required Catholics to take an oath of loyalty.

Catholic Relief Act, 1791
Catholics ceased to be liable to prosecution for their faith. The registration of Catholic estates was ended; the legal profession was opened to Catholics. Catholic places of worship, and their schools, had to be registered, and thus became legal. It ceased to be illegal to send children to continental Roman Catholic seminaries to be educated.

Catholic Emancipation Act, 1829
Catholics ceased to be disabled from sitting in Parliament or holding public office.

FURTHER READING
Much information on the penal laws is provided by:

• Anstey, Thomas Chisholme. *A Guide to the Laws of England affecting Roman Catholics.* V. & R. Stevens, & G.S. Norton, 1842.

See also:

• Madden, R.R. *The History of the Penal Laws enacted against Roman Catholics, the Operation and Results of that System of Legalised Plunder, Persecution, and Proscription, originating in Rapacity and Fraudulent Designs, concealed under False Pretences, Figments of Reform, and a Simulated Zeal for the Interests of True Religion.* Thomas Richardson & Son, 1847.

The laws as experienced by Catholics under Charles II and earlier are discussed by:

• Williams, J.A. 'English Catholicism under Charles II: the legal position', *Recusant History* 7, 1963, p.123-43.

B. THE RECORDS: GENERAL
Clerks of the Peace and diocesan registrars kept archives relating to the persecution of Catholics. So did the Court of Exchequer and other central government bodies. Fines, imprisonment and capital punishment could only be imposed by secular courts: usually either Quarter Sessions (in both counties and boroughs), or Assizes, but sometimes also the central courts. The collection of fines was the responsibility of sheriffs, who accounted for them at the Exchequer. The Secretaries of State regularly received information from both ecclesiastical and secular courts concerning the prevalence of recusancy in their areas. Other documents relating to recusancy were created by the Forfeited Estates Commission, and by a variety of other central government organizations.

Much of this material is only briefly described in catalogues, and is unindexed. It is therefore necessary to identify documents dealing with topics which may potentially be relevant to your research, and to search them speculatively. Hopefully, the information given below will help you to do this. The class numbers given below relate to documents in the National Archives. For a general introduction to official sources for tracing recusants, see:

• Shorney, David. *Protestant Nonconformity and Roman Catholicism: a guide to sources in the Public Record Office*. PRO Publications, 1996.

A more detailed guide is provided by:

• Williams, J. Anthony. *Sources for Recusant History (1559-1791) in English Official Archives*. Catholic Record Society, 1983. Published as *Recusant history*, 16(4), 1983.

C. THE RECORDS: CHURCH OF ENGLAND DIOCESAN ARCHIVES
Visitation Records

Recusants first came to the notice of the ecclesiastical courts through churchwardens' presentments made at visitation. Visitation records can therefore be particularly useful.[10] Bishops and archdeacons conducted regular visitations of their jurisdictions, investigating (among many other topics) the prevalence of Catholicism. Prior to visitations, bishops sometimes sent out preliminary queries. Originally, these were intended to guide churchwardens in the compilation of their presentments. However, churchwardens' slackness led to queries being directed to the clergy from the late seventeenth century. Detailed questions were asked. In 1821, for example, Bishop Carey of Exeter asked: 'have you any Papists or Dissenters? If the latter, of what kind or denomination? What teachers of each are there resident in your parish, or occasionally visiting it? Are they licensed? What places have they of public meeting, licensed or otherwise?' The answers to such questions obviously provide much valuable information about Catholicism. The return for Stourton (Wiltshire) in 1783 reveals that there was a Roman Catholic chapel in the parish catering for at last a hundred worshippers, that its priest, who had been there for fifteen or sixteen years, had recently died, and that the Papists had 'a woman's school for children'. Many 'replies to queries' have been published by county record societies.[11] For the answers of Anglican clergy to a question about Catholics in the Diocese of York, see:

• Trappes-Lomax, Richard, ed. 'Archbishop Blackburn's visitation returns of the Diocese of York, 1735', in *Miscellanea* [15]. Catholic Record Society 32. 1932, p. 204-388.

Presentments

Visitation queries sent to churchwardens were intended to guide them in the compilation of presentments. These presentments were sometimes sent in before visitations commenced,[12] and digests of them were made for the court. Alternatively, they might be presented orally, and written down by court officials. They reported on a wide range of issues, of which recusancy was only one.

Churchwardens were best placed to know what was going on in their churches, and to identify those who refused to attend. They did not like presenting their neighbours, although they were legally obligated to do so. Many concealed offences or made inaccurate presentments. Churchwardens from no fewer than seventeen parishes at the Archbishop of York's 1632–33 visitation were charged with neglecting to make true presentments.[13] In 1680, the Bishop of Peterborough complained that 'defects will never be known by the presentment of the churchwardens'.[14] Sometimes, 'informations' made by Court apparitors bypassed the need for churchwardens' presentments.

The presentment of recusants was spasmodic. Perhaps the most were made after 1660, when churchwardens were enthusiastic about the Restoration settlement. Presentments for religious offences constituted half of the presentments made in the Peterborough court between 1662 and 1664. In 1662, no fewer than forty-seven individuals 'conceaved to be Popishly affected' were presented to the Archdeaconry court by the churchwardens of Stourton (Wiltshire). At the same time, only nineteen Stourton recusants were presented to Quarter Sessions by the constables of the Hundred of Mere.[15]

The enthusiasm displayed by churchwardens in the wake of the Restoration was not shared by Charles II's government, nor was it to last. Increasingly, churchwardens failed to report the sins of their neighbours, despite the bishops' queries. Later presentments from Stourton contained few or no recusant names. Lack of evidence of recusants in presentments is no evidence that recusants were not present.

Presentments for religious reasons ceased after James II's Declaration of Indulgence in 1687, and the Toleration Act 1689, both of which suspended the laws against non-attendance at church (although they did not actually repeal them).

For a collection of Worcestershire presentments, see

• Lascelles, Lillian, & Guise-Barrow, E. 'Churchwardens' Presentments 1664–1768', *Worcestershire Recusant* 4-23, 1964-74, passim.

For lists of recusants from Archbishop Laud's visitation of the Diocese of Coventry and Lichfield, see:

• Wanklyn, Malcolm. 'Shropshire recusants in 1635', *Midland Catholic History* 3, 1994, p.8-14.
• Hampartumian, Jane. 'Staffordshire recusants in 1635', *Staffordshire Catholic History* 22, 1984, p.5-23

Names from Bishop Hacket's visitation of 1665, and from the visitations of various peculiars, 1668–70, are listed in:

• Hampartumian, J. 'Staffordshire recusants in the 1660s', *Staffordshire Catholic History* 23, 1988, p.14-27.

Citations, Detections, other Court Records, and Marriage

Citations to appear in archdeaconry courts may help to identify recusants. Annotations may indicate the nature of the cases against them, but that is not always the case. In the case of Stourton (Wiltshire), it has been possible to identify a substantial number of recusants from citations in the 1630s, but only because many individuals were cited together, and some could be identified from other sources as recusants. Citations may be recorded in act books; for example, those from the Elizabethan Diocese of Winchester record numerous citations, despite the fact that visitation records yield little information concerning Catholicism. Act books may also record other information about recusants; for example, sentences. Some extracts from an act book are published in:

• Hansom, J.S., ed. 'Recusants of Masham, Yorkshire', *Miscellanea 3*.
Catholic Record Society 3. 1906, p.82-6.

Specific accusations, termed 'detections', were sometimes gathered
together in a volume of 'detecta' or 'comperta' after visitations. A
variety of other sources may also be available. For example, a 1604
survey of Yorkshire recusants reports that:

> Richard Cholmley Esquier maryed with Mary Hungate in the
> presence of John Wilson, William Martin, Hugh Hope & Christopher
> Danyell in a fell with a popishe priest, as they here.[16]

Cholmley had evidently not felt safe to have a Catholic priest in his
house, so he and his bride were married on a lonely Yorkshire fell in
secret. No entry was made in the parish register, and the celebrant
probably kept no record; the event was reported as hearsay.

After about 1590, prosecutions for clandestine marriage increased.
Catholics could claim their marriages were valid under common law,[17]
but might nevertheless be prosecuted in the ecclesiastical courts for
failing to comply with the canonical requirement that marriage should
be conducted in their parish church, and preceded by banns. They might
alternatively be accused of fornication.

Roman Catholics can sometimes also be traced through records of
penances, excommunications and bonds. When excommunication
failed to impress the convicted, the church could call in the aid of the
secular courts, and send a signification of excommunication to the Court
of Chancery.[18] These significations are now in various classes in the
National Archives: 1220-1611 (class C85), 1727-76, and 1842-3 (class
C207/1-12 & 23). For Cheshire, some significations, 1378-1690 (with
gaps) are in CHES 38/25/4-6.

Court of High Commission

The Court of High Commission was the supreme ecclesiastical court in
England between around 1560 and 1640. It enforced ecclesiastical
discipline throughout the country. From 1558, it had powers to fine and
imprison not enjoyed by other ecclesiastical courts. It instigated
disciplinary procedures against those whose social position might
render them immune to prosecution in other courts. It was particularly

concerned with recusancy, but dealt with the whole range of topics covered by ecclesiastical courts. Archbishop Laud used it against puritanism; consequently, it was abolished by the Long Parliament.

In practice, separate high commissions operated in the two provinces. The majority of High Commission records for the Southern Province do not survive. However, a few can be found in the National Archives, classes E12/5 & 7-10 and E135/13/1-5, covering 1595 to 1637. Court books can sometimes be found among diocesan archives. For example, the court's register for Kent, 1584–1603, records that it dealt with twenty-two prominent Kent Catholics between 1572 and 1603.[19]

Many High Commission act books and other court papers from the Northern Province are deposited at the Borthwick Institute **https:// borthcat.york.ac.uk/index.php/archiepiscopal-courts**. Their use is demonstrated by McClain's discussion of how the Boroughbridge (Yorkshire) Catholics tried to force out their Protestant vicar and his clerk in 1597, and by Aveling's discussion of Catholic marriages challenged by the Commission.[20] For their significance, see:

• Tyler, Philip. 'The Significance of the Ecclesiastical Commission at York', *Northern History* 2, 1967, p.27-44.
• Manning, Roger B. 'Elizabethan Recusancy commissions', *Historical Journal* 15(1), 1972, p.23-36.

For extracts from the act and deposition books of the High Commission in Co. Durham, 1628–39, see:

• Longstaffe, W.H.D., ed. *The Acts of the High Commission Court within the Diocese of Durham.* Surtees Society 34. 1857. Covers 1628-39.

Governmental Censuses of Roman Catholics

The government was particularly concerned to know how many Catholics there were. Bishops' queries, discussed above, frequently elicited statistical information. Many lists of recusants' names can also be found elsewhere. Most counts were made by bishops, although they might also be undertaken by Justices of the Peace or Lord Lieutenants. Most of those mentioned here cover the whole country, but there are others which only deal with particular dioceses or counties.[21] These censuses are particularly useful for pinpointing places where Catholics were active.

The earliest attempt at a national census was a very hurried affair in 1577. Bishops had little time to compile detailed lists. Consequently, there are many obvious omissions; for example, the Salisbury returns do not even mention the hotbed of recusancy at Stourton. The returns are now in class SP 12/117-9, and are printed in:

• Ryan, Patrick, ed. 'Diocesan Returns of Recusants for England and Wales, 1577', in *Miscellanea 12*. Catholic Record Society 22. 1921, p.1-114.

In 1586, as the threat of Spanish invasion loomed, lists were drawn up of those thought likely to aid the Spanish. These are in the State Papers, SP 12/191/22, SP 12/193/13, and SP 12/ 193/47.

The revised canons of 1603 made provision for an annual census of Catholics to be taken. A statistical return without names for 1603 is in the British Library, Harleian Mss 280, f.157-62. A number of nominal returns from this census also survive. Perhaps the listing made by the Yorkshire Justices of the Peace in 1604, listing 2,461 names, was a return from this census;[22] it is printed in:

• Peacock, Edward, ed. *A list of the Roman Catholics in the County of York in 1604*. John Camden Hotten, 1872.

Another census was taken in 1676, although this was mainly statistical. It has been printed as:

• Whiteman, Anne, ed. *The Compton census of 1676: a critical edition.* Records of social and economic history new series 10. Oxford University Press, 1986.

For Lancashire, some names were recorded. See:

• Pannikkar, Margaret, ed. *The Compton Census of 1676: the Lancashire Returns.* North West Catholic History Society, 1995.

For an analysis of this census and its accuracy from the Catholic point of view, see:

- 'The Catholics of 1676 as recorded in the Compton Census', in Rowlands, Marie B., ed. *English Catholics of Parish and Town 1558-1778*. Catholic Record Society, 1999, p.78-114.

In 1680, lists of Catholics were compiled for a 'Papists (Removal and Disarming) Bill', which never passed. These lists are in the Parliamentary Archives,[23] which also holds a 1689 return of Catholics living in Westminster and the London suburbs, taken with a view to removing them ten miles from London.[24] The papers of the Earl of Shaftesbury, which have been deposited in the National Archives, include a return of Papists in Dorset during the reign of Charles II (PRO30/24/7/530).

In 1705 and 1706, several different authorities requested statistical information on recusants. A few returns made by deputy lieutenants and bishops are in the Parliamentary Archives.[25] Returns to the Bishop of Lichfield and Coventry are printed in:

- Greenslade, M.W. 'Staffordshire Papists in 1705 and 1706', *Staffordshire Catholic History* 13, 1973, 1-55.

In 1706, an Order in Council required bishops 'to take an Exact and Particular Account of the Number of the papists and Reputed Papists in every Parish, with their Qualities Estates and Places of Abode'.[26] Again, returns are held by the Parliamentary Archives, although some county returns are missing. Published returns are listed by:

- British Religion in Statistics: Census of the numbers and (often) the names and occupations of Roman Catholics (2531)
  www.brin.ac.uk/sources/2531/

For a discussion of the returns for one county, see:

- Williams, J.A. 'Wiltshire Catholicism in the Early Eighteenth Century; the diocesan returns of 1706', *Recusant History*, 7(1), 1963, p.11-22.

Another attempt to conduct a census of Roman Catholics in England and Wales took place in 1767, when the House of Lords asked the Crown to give Directions to the Archbishops and Bishops, to procure from their Parochial Clergy ... as correct and complete Lists as can be obtained of the Papists, or reputed Papists, within the same; distinguishing their Parishes, Sexes, Ages, and Occupations, and how long they have been there resident.

The returns are printed in:

• Worrall, E.S. ed. *Returns of Papists 1767.* 2 vols. Catholic Record Society Occasional Publications, 1-2. 1980-89. Vol. 1. Diocese of Chester. Vol. 2. Dioceses of England and Wales, except Chester.

See also:

• 'Returns of Papists 1767', *Catholic Ancestor* 3(1), 1990, p.22-5.

For a discussion of the reliability and uses of the 1767 returns, see:

• 'Part III: Catholics on the Eve of the Relief Acts', in Rowlands, Marie B., ed. *English Catholics of parish and Town 1558-1778.* Catholic Record Society, 1999, p.261-352.

The final governmental attempt to conduct a census solely concerned with Roman Catholics was made in 1780. Unfortunately, the summaries of returns held in the Parliamentary Archives mostly lack names, although they occasionally mention Catholic schools. Statistics are available for most parishes, apart from those in the dioceses of Llandaff, Oxford, and Bath & Wells. A total of 69,376 Papists were counted. More detailed parish returns, sometimes including names, may sometimes be found among Anglican Diocesan archives.

In the nineteenth century, the government twice attempted to count places of worship: in 1829, and again in 1851. The returns enable us to determine the number of Roman Catholics. In 1829, the focus was on non-Anglican places.

Unfortunately, the majority of returns have been lost; however, a few do survive, including the printed return for Lancashire. For details, see:

- Ambler, R.W. 'A lost Source? The 1829 Returns of non-Anglican places of worship', *Local Historian* 17(08), 1987, p.403-9.

The 1851 religious census included all places of worship. Its published reports give the total numbers of places of worship and attenders for the whole country. For digitised reproductions of the returns, visit:

- British Religion in Numbers: Religious Census 1851 Online **www.brin.ac.uk/2010/religious-census-1851-online**

The original returns (class HO 129) provide information on each individual place of worship, including the numbers attending all services on 30 March 1851, the number of free seats available, the dates chapels were erected, and other comments from incumbents. Worshippers' names are not recorded. Returns were signed by priests or church officers; the latter sometimes indicated their occupations.

These returns provide much more accurate statistics than the censuses discussed above. They do, however, pose the problem that, where two or more worship services were conducted on the same day, it is impossible to determine how many people attended both services.

A detailed study is provided by:

- Snell, K.D.M., & Ell, Paul S. *Rival Jerusalems: the geography of Victorian religion.* Cambridge University Press, 2000.

For analysis of one county's returns, see:

- Wolffe, J. *The Religious Census of 1851 in Yorkshire.* Borthwick Papers, 108. Borthwick Institute, 2005.

Guides to the 1851 census are provided by:

- Thompson, David M. 'The religious census of 1851', in Lawton, Richard, ed. *The census and social structure: an interpretative guide to nineteenth-century censuses for England and Wales.* Frank Cass, 1978, p.241-88.

• Field, Clive D. 'The 1851 Religious Census of Great Britain: a bibliographical guide for Local and Regional Historians', *Local Historian* 27(4), 1997, p.194-217.

The government was not alone in wanting to count Roman Catholics. The Catholic hierarchy also needed this information, and made various efforts to collect it. The resultant documentation is discussed below, p.177–8.

D. QUARTER SESSIONS, ASSIZES, AND THE CENTRAL COURTS

Most recusants were prosecuted at Quarter Sessions, except during the brief period noted below. Assizes heard cases that had been passed on to them by Quarter Sessions. Cases could also be removed to the central courts, and especially to the Court of King's Bench, by writs of *certiorari*.

County record offices were originally established to preserve the records of Quarter Sessions. The records of King's Bench are preserved in the National Archives. So are the records of the Assize courts, although, sadly, few survive before the eighteenth century. A detailed introduction to the records of Assizes and Quarter Sessions is provided by:

• Raymond, Stuart A. *Tracing your Ancestors in County Records: a guide for Family and Local Historians.* Pen & Sword, 2016.

For a summary listing of surviving Quarter Sessions records, see:

• Gibson, Jeremy. *Quarter Sessions records for Family Historians.* 5th ed. Family History Partnership, 2007.

Quarter Sessions

Roman Catholics usually came to the notice of the secular courts by presentment, although indictments and informations could also result in prosecution. After the Act of 1581, the Archbishop of Canterbury directed his diocesans to ensure that churchwardens furnished lists of recusants before each Quarter Sessions and Assizes, so that indictments could be made.[27] Presentments could be made by parish constables, churchwardens (after 1605), Justices of the Peace, or by the Grand Jury. Informers also had a role.[28] Perhaps only one in three or one in four presentments led to conviction.

Presentments and indictments indicate hostility towards Roman Catholicism, not its prevalence. Their absence does not mean there were no Roman Catholics. Constables and others responsible for making presentments could be sympathetic to Catholicism, or even active Roman Catholics themselves. Presentments were not always made willingly: in 1604, Thomas Herbert, the Lord Mayor of York, was forced to join in the accusation made against his brother Christopher, who was described as 'sometymes remayning at ye lord Maior his house, but cometh not to church: recusant'. Men such as Herbert avoided making presentments if they could.

Those accused of recusancy had to enter recognizances (bonds) promising to appear in court, under financial penalty if they did not. Justices of the Peace also used them to bind convicted recusants to 'good behaviour'. That was interpreted as meaning to keep the peace, rather than to conform. Many recognizances survive, and may provide useful information.

As the number of prosecutions increased after the passing of the 1581 Act, so did the number of evasions. Suspicion of leniency fell on Justices of the Peace, and consequently recusancy ceased to be triable at Quarter Sessions in 1586 (presentments could still be made there). Jurisdiction was transferred to the Assizes, and to the King's Bench. Conviction became automatic if the accused failed to appear. Occasionally, government appointed special commissions to investigate recusancy.[29] Jurisdiction was restored to Quarter Sessions in 1606, although the Assizes could still be involved.

With the exception of the period from 1586 to 1606, convictions were recorded in Quarter Sessions order books. These also record matters such as registration of Catholic property, general directives of the court concerning Catholics and orders from central government. Recusant convictions were recorded in estreats sent to the Exchequer, notifying the fines and forfeitures imposed by the court. These are discussed below, p.86. There may be other records; for example, in the North Riding separate books of 'recusants indicted' were kept from 1611.[30]

Most cases against Catholics heard at Quarter Sessions were for recusancy. There were comparatively few for matters such as hearing mass, refusing the oath of allegiance or being an unlicensed schoolmaster. However, during the Interregnum, prosecutions for recusancy virtually ceased. Instead, under an Act of 1657, recusants were required to take the oath of abjuration. The penalty for refusing to do so was sequestration of two-thirds of the offender's property.

The extent of prosecution varied considerably from county to county, and from year to year. Much depended on political developments and the level of the perceived threat from Catholics. Thus a Parliamentary inquiry in 1640 led to a surge of prosecutions, whereas the lack of prosecutions during the early years of Charles II's reign considerably reduced the government's income from recusancy fines. Proceedings frequently depended on whom the offender knew. Queen Elizabeth frequently intervened; for example, when she heard that Lady Stourton was threatened with proceedings in 1601, she immediately had them stayed.[31]

Imprisoned recusants may be listed in calendars of prisoners, which were sometimes endorsed with sentences and other orders of the court, and frequently used as wrappers for sessions rolls.

Many Quarter Sessions records are in print.[32] A useful general introduction to these records is included in:

• Peyton, S.A., ed. *Minutes of proceedings in Quarter Sessions held for the Parts of Kesteven in the County of Lincoln, 1674-1695.* Vol.1. Lincoln Record Society 25. 1931.

Many indictments, recognizances, jury panels and other documents relating to the conviction of recusants in London have been brought together in:

• Bowler, Hugh, ed. *London Sessions Records, 1605-1685.* Catholic Record Society 34. 1934.

For a list of indicted recusants in Staffordshire at the outbreak of the Civil War, see:

• Kettle, Ann J. 'A list of Staffordshire Recusants 1641', *Staffordshire Catholic History,* 5, 1964, p.1-37.

A register of recusants found among Lancashire Quarter Sessions records is printed in:

• Gardner, Norman, ed. *Lancashire Quarter Sessions records: register of recusants 1678*. North West Catholic History Society, 1998. There are similar volumes for 1679 and 1682.

For a detailed 'list of recusants presented in 1611' in the North Riding, see:

• Atkinson, J.C., ed. *Quarter Sessions Records, vol.3*. North Riding Record Society, 1885, p.60-108. Many other recusant presentments are recorded in other volumes of this series.

For a list of Staffordshire men summoned to take the oath of abjuration or face conviction as recusants, see:

• Greenslade, Michael, ed. 'List of Staffordshire Recusants 1657, transcribed from Manuscript Q/RRr among the Quarter Sessions Records in the Staffordshire Record Office', *Staffordshire Record Society* 4th series, 2. 1958, p.71-99

The names of Monmouthshire recusants proceeded against in 1719 are listed in a Quarter Sessions process book:

• Matthews, John Hobson. 'Monmouthshire recusants, 1719', in *Miscellanea VI: Bedingfield papers &c*. Catholic Record Society, 7. 1909, p.246-54.

Lists of Catholics prosecuted at Quarter Sessions can turn up in odd places. For late seventeenth-century lists of West Riding prosecutions, see:

• Turner, J. Horsfall, ed. *The Nonconformist Register of Baptisms, Marriages and Deaths compiled by the Revs. Oliver Heywood & T. Dickenson, 1644-1702, 1702-1752, generally known as the Northowram or Coley register, but comprehending numerous notices of Puritans and anti-Puritans in Yorkshire, Lancashire, Cheshire, London, &c., with lists of popish recusants, Quakers,* etc. J.S.Jowett, 1881, p.117-31 &157-63.

Assizes

Itinerant Assize judges exercised general supervision over Justices of the Peace and Quarter Sessions. They ensured that government policy towards recusants was implemented locally, and the charges they delivered in court reflected their instructions from the Crown. In the 1630s, for example, the judges of the Northern Circuit insisted that the levy of 12d for each Sunday's absence should be collected.[33]

Assize records are preserved in the National Archives, in the ASSI classes. Unfortunately, comparatively few pre-1800 records survive. Only one circuit has a complete set of indictments from Elizabeth's reign. Fortunately, the missing information can frequently be found in Quarter Sessions records, Privy Council registers and other sources. Estreats recording fines and forfeitures imposed by the Assizes, like those imposed by Quarter Sessions, were sent to the Exchequer, and recorded in the Recusant rolls (see below, p.85–90).

Most surviving sixteenth and seventeenth-century records in the ASSI classes are in print. Cockburn has calendared many volumes of sixteenth and seventeenth-century Assize records for Essex, Hertfordshire, Kent, Surrey, Sussex and the Western Circuit. These frequently refer to Catholics. See, for example:

• Cockburn, J.S., ed. *Calendar of Assize Records: Essex Indictments Elizabeth I.* HMSO, 1978.

A number of other editions of Assize records are available. For example, there are many lists of recusants indicted at the York Assizes in:

• [Raine, James], ed. *Depositions from the Castle of York, relating to offences committed in the Northern Counties in the Seventeenth Century.* Surtees Society, 40. 1861.

Assize records for the Palatinate of Chester are separated from the main ASSI classes in the National Archives. These include Crown books (CHES 21) and plea rolls (CHES 29) dating from the 1580s. They record many indictments of recusants, and list numerous Catholic prisoners.

Two National Archives guides are devoted to Assize records:

- How to look for records of ... Criminal Trials in the Assize Courts 1559-1971
www.nationalarchives.gov.uk/help-with-your-research/research-guides/criminal-trials-assize-courts-1559-1971
- How to look for records of... Criminal trials in the English assize courts 1559-1971 – key to records
www.nationalarchives.gov.uk/help-with-your-research/research-guides/criminal-trials-english-assize-courts-1559-1971-key-to-records

King's Bench

King's Bench was the principal common law court. Its records are in the National Archives. Many cases concerning Catholics, which began at Quarter Sessions or Assizes, were transferred to King's Bench by writ of *certiorari*. Other cases might be begun there. For criminal prosecutions, defendants are initially traceable through the controlment rolls, KB 29, which record the progress of Crown Cases from term to term, and serve as a means of reference to the Coram Rege rolls (KB 27), or, after 1702, the Crown Rolls (KB 28). These include many writs to sheriffs for the arrest of obstinate excommunicants, as well as records of fines, forfeitures and other proceedings. Many indictments in KB 9-11 relate to prosecutions of priests, recusants, mass attenders and, after 1715, Jacobites. Between 1661 and 1733 there is a register of indictments and informations (KB 15/58), which makes reference to the indictment files easier. The *Baga de Secretis* (KB 8) includes the official records of Jacobite trials after the 1715 and 1745 rebellions. Similar records are in KB 33.

A number of documents which had nothing to do with proceedings in the court found their way to King's Bench. Among these are a few certificates of conformity among the *Recorda* files, KB 145. These certificates were obtained by those who wished to free themselves from any accusation of recusancy. They give names, domiciles, dates and occasionally other information. These certificates are difficult to use; however, they have been calendared for the period 1563–1627 by:

- Clarke, Dorothy M. 'Conformity Certificates among the King's Bench Records: a Calendar', *Recusant History*, 14(1), 1977, p. 53 -63.

For more detailed guides to the extensive King's Bench records, see:

- How to look for records of... Court of King's Bench records 1200-1600
  www.nationalarchives.gov.uk/help-with-your-research/ research-guides/court-kings-bench-records-1200-1600
- How to look for records of Court of King's Bench (Crown Side) cases 1675-1875
  www.nationalarchives.gov.uk/help-with-your-research/ research-guides/court-kings-bench-crown-side-1675-1875

Star Chamber

Star Chamber was the judicial arm of the King's Council until it was abolished in 1641. Riot and affray were the keynote of many of its proceedings. Such affray could occur as a result of resistance to the seizure of Catholic goods, to interference with Catholic marriages or burial rites, or to the protection given to Catholic priests. The words 'riot and affray' can cover a multitude of actions in which Catholics were involved. However, the available indexes rarely directly mention recusancy; it is necessary to search them for the names of known Catholics. For a detailed guide to Star Chamber records, see:

- How to look for Court of Star Chamber records 1485-1642
  www.nationalarchives.gov.uk/help-with-your-research/ research-guides/court-star-chamber-records-1485-1642

An important index to Star Chamber proceedings (class STAC) is provided by:

- Barnes, T.G., ed. *List and Index to the Proceedings in Star Chamber for the Reign of James I in the Public Record Office.* 3 vols. (Chicago, 1975)

E. THE EXCHEQUER, 1. RECUSANT ROLLS AND COMPOUNDING

Between 1581 and 1691, as has already been seen, anyone who failed to attend their parish church was liable to substantial fines. Under the 1586 Act, those who failed to pay could forfeit their goods and two-thirds of their lands. Under the act of 1593, they could also forfeit copyhold property. Those who refused to take the oath of allegiance were subjected to forfeiture of lands under the Act of 1610. Failure to appear in court when cited meant automatic conviction of recusancy.

The Clerk of the Peace, or the Clerk of Assize, made estreats listing convictions and penalties imposed, and sent them to the Exchequer.[34] These estreats are now in classes E 137 and E 362. The Exchequer instructed sheriffs to collect these fines, and to account for them. The process was recorded on the Pipe Rolls (class E 372/426-436) between 1581 and 1592.[35] The 1586 Act, as already noted, had 'clarified' the 1581 Act by making it clear that only one conviction was required in order for a recusant to become liable to regular monthly fines. This meant that those who had assumed a conviction merely involved a payment of one £20 monthly fine found themselves sadly mistaken. They had in fact accumulated hefty outstanding fines since 1581, and very few were able to clear them immediately.[36] By 1592, 266 recusants had had their lands distrained for failure to pay.[37] However, until an Act of 1593,[38] payment of fines and forfeitures imposed on wives convicted of recusancy could not be enforced; in common law, they had no property of their own, and their husbands had no liability for their fines and forfeitures. However, if the wife was committed to gaol for non-payment, her husband could obtain her release by paying her fines. Otherwise, payment could only be enforced when wives became widows. There are many examples of forfeitures being imposed following the deaths of husbands.[39]

In 1592, the increasing bulk of the Pipe Rolls resulted in the creation of a separate series of Recusant Rolls. However, fines imposed on Catholics for offences other than recusancy continued to appear in the Pipe Rolls, which may therefore still be worth examination. The recusant rolls were (with a few gaps) compiled annually from 1593 until 1691, and are in class E 376. Duplicates of the series are in E 377. These record the fines and forfeitures for which the Exchequer was responsible.

Arrangement of the rolls is by county. There are, however, peculiarities in the arrangement. London and Middlesex are frequently bracketed together. So are Surrey and Sussex, and Yorkshire and Durham. Yorkshire appears as *Ebor*, Hampshire as Southampton and Worcestershire as *Wigorn*. All the Welsh counties are entered at the end of each roll under the single heading *Wallia*. Entries under London, Middlesex, and Surrey frequently include the names of recusants from other counties.

These rolls were compiled from Michaelmas to Michaelmas, rather than being dated by regnal years, that is, by the date of the monarch's accession. This must be taken into account when comparing the information in them with information in documents such as the Memoranda Rolls (see below, p.93).

The process at the Exchequer began with the entry of the estreat on the rolls, and the issue of process to the sheriff. Entries are not always as accurate as they should be; the details had been copied at least three times by the time the estreats reached the Exchequer. Names and placenames are, therefore, occasionally misspelt.[40] Estreats record recusants' names and addresses, periods of recusancy and dates of conviction.

The rolls themselves were written in Latin, except during the Interregnum. Entries follow a standard format.[41] Most of them relate to forfeitures of land (which give much detail), and to the collection of £20 fines (which are entered last, merely naming recusants and amounts due). Entries generally begin with a preamble, followed by rentals of seized lands, details of seized goods and chattels, sheriff's charges and estreats of convictions. There may also be details of fines for offences such as attendance at mass.

Entries relating to the rentals of seized lands give details of the property and the names of Crown lessees (if any), together with financial details such as arrears of payment, the total debt and payments made. This information may be followed by records of the seizure of goods and chattels, sometimes mentioning particular items seized. There are relatively few references to revenue received from such seizures. This is probably due to the fact that there was much peculation when seized goods were auctioned. Such entries as were made rarely provide much information concerning the goods seized.[42] Sometimes reference is made to the authorization for seizure entered on the Memoranda Rolls (E 159). In view of the fact that forfeitures resulted in recurrent income, they were re-enrolled, in abbreviated form, in the rolls of subsequent years. Consequently, it is possible to trace Exchequer action against specific recusants through the rolls for many years.

Many entries relate to Exchequer procedure, and to the way in which sheriffs accounted for their activities, including statements of sheriff's charges and arrears. Sometimes, these indicate that specific 'debts' were to be carried forward to the following year, and not collected.[43]

Estreats of convictions are abbreviated versions of indictments from Quarter Sessions and Assizes. They give the recusant's name, parish, rank or occupation, the period of recusancy, the date of conviction, the amount of the fine and the date when the estreat was despatched to the Exchequer. Frequently they are recorded in recusant rolls two or three years earlier in date than the conviction. Once such an entry is found, it is necessary to search a roll of a date at least a year later than the conviction to find details of seizures, and subsequent rolls to trace the amounts mulcted from the recusant from year to year.

Once details of convictions had been entered on the rolls, commissioners had to be appointed to investigate and value recusants' lands by the judgement of juries appointed by the sheriff. In the early years the Exchequer was overwhelmed by the number of recusants and frequently failed to issue commissions. Some recusants were convicted and enrolled on a number of occasions before commissions were issued. The threat that goods might be confiscated could be used to hold recusants *in terrorem*. The convictions of poor recusants were frequently not entered on the rolls at all. Even when commissioners were appointed, juries were quite likely to return a value of nil. A West Riding jury, presented with a list of forty-six recusants for investigation in 1589, reported that only fourteen of them had property worth seizing.[44] The details returned were entered onto the recusant roll, which may even include a transcription of the jurors' actual verdicts. If lands were seized, they were described, and the date of distraint was given, together with details of the rent due to the Crown, and the names of commissioners who executed seizure. Distraint was, however, a slow process, and might be delayed for many years, or not executed at all. The government administered the land – usually by making twenty-one year leases – and took the rents until fines were paid.[45]

The purpose of fining and forfeiture was to extract as much money as possible from the recusant community, with the minimum expense. In the decade after the passage of the 1586 Act, revenue averaged over £6,000 per year; in 1600–01 it totalled over £9,000.[46] Fines and forfeitures fell primarily on property owners. The wage-earning poor were largely ignored, as the cost of pursuing them might be greater than the revenue to be derived. Many of the greater gentry and the aristocracy were able to obtain letters of protection exempting them from fining, or escaped by using good lawyers. Fines and forfeitures therefore fell primarily on the lesser gentry.[47]

Forfeiture was not always as onerous as it could have been. Title to seized lands remained with convicted recusants; it was merely the revenue that was forfeited. Penalties could be reduced by clever lawyers. The strict settlement, which gave landowners merely a life interest in property, and the use of trusts which placed ownership in the hands of Protestant relatives and friends, could limit the amount available for seizure.[48]

Sometimes the recusant continued to receive his rents, but handed them over to the sheriff.[49] Crown lessees of recusant lands sometimes sub-let them to their owners' conforming relatives or friends.[50] There were many ways in which the impact of recusant penalties could be mitigated.

During the Civil War and Interregnum, collection of fines by the Exchequer gradually ceased, and the grounds for conviction changed. In the absence of an established church, church attendance could not be enforced. In 1643, refusal to take an oath of abjuration became the basis for recusancy convictions. The collection of fines frequently became a matter for Parliamentary County Committees, rather than the Exchequer. Entries on the recusant rolls gradually diminished, although those who had already been convicted continued to pay their fines. There are no rolls for 1650, 1652 and 1653. A 1655 proclamation, confirmed by an Act of 1657, made refusal of an oath denouncing the Pope equivalent to recusancy.[51] Convictions resumed. So did collection of fines by the Exchequer, and the compilation of recusant rolls.

After 1660, the recusancy laws were applied very erratically, and the recusant rolls record only a small number of entries. Revenue fell to £2,000 in 1683–4, and to a mere £384 in 1684–5[52]. Fines ceased to be imposed in 1687, although arrears continued to be collected until 1691. Instead, recusants liable to the land tax (see below, p.99–100) were required to pay double.

Not only Catholics were recusants. Nonconformists were too, if they refused to attend services of the established church. Some of the names found on recusant rolls may be theirs. They were few in number before 1662, but in subsequent rolls they may even outnumber Roman Catholics. The treatment of Nonconformists varied across the country; many appeared in the Wiltshire recusant rolls, but none in those for Cheshire and Shropshire.[53]

A number of recusant rolls have been published by the Catholic Record Society. The earliest entries in the Pipe Rolls are included in:

- Bowler, Hugh, & McCann, Timothy J., eds. *Recusants in the Exchequer Pipe Rolls 1581–1592.* Catholic Record Society, 71. 1986.

Published recusant rolls proper include:

- Calthrop, M.M.C., ed. *Recusant roll No. 1. 1592-3. Exchequer, Lord Treasurer's Remembrancer, Pipe Office series.* Catholic Record Society 18. 1916.
- Bowler, Hugh, ed. *Recusant roll no.2 (1593-1594): an abstract in English.* Catholic Record Society 57. 1965.
- Bowler, Hugh, ed. *Recusant roll no.3 (1594-1595) and recusant roll no.4 (1595-1596).* Catholic Record Society 60. 1968.
- LaRocca, John, ed. *Jacobean Recusant rolls for Middlesex: an abstract in English.* Catholic Record Society 76. 1997.

The recusant rolls for the Interregnum period have been microfilmed as reels 22–5 of:

- *Unpublished State Papers of the English Civil War and Interregnum.* Microfilm. (Harvester Press, 1975-8).

For general guides to the recusant rolls, see:

- Bowler, Hugh. 'Some notes on the recusant rolls of the Exchequer', *Recusant History* 4(5), 1958, p.182-98. See also 4(6), 1958, p.243-4.
- Williams, J.A. 'Recusant rolls', in Munby, Lionel M., ed. *Short guides to records.* Historical Association, 1972.

Compositions for Recusancy
Very few recusants could afford to pay their fines; indeed, they were not expected to. Rather, the legislation was used to ensure that they were kept in a permanent state of indebtedness to the Crown. The government tried to keep a balance between extracting as much revenue from them as possible, while enabling them to maintain regular payments. Fines were compounded: that is, reduced to a level that was affordable, on condition that payments were regularly made. This not only ensured that recusants had sufficient income to live in a way befitting their status, but was also thought to reduce evasion and to

ensure that the government had a reliable source of regular income. Fines became a source of income to the Crown, rather than a means of extirpating Catholicism from England.

Tentative steps towards compounding were taken in 1586.[54] It was not, however, until the seventeenth century that compounding became the norm. Experiments in compounding were again made in 1614, 1619 and 1625. In 1627 two permanent commissions were established: one in Westminster, the other in York. They succeeded in increasing the value of recusancy fines from just over £6,000 per year in 1631 to £32,000 in 1640.[55] Catholics paid more for their faith under Charles I than they had under either Elizabeth or James I. That probably accounts for their reluctance to join his army during the Civil War.

The Commissioners granted leases of lands seized from recusants (frequently to the recusants themselves), and collected outstanding recusancy fines. The compositions they sought to impose were based on how much the Commissioners believed recusants could afford to pay without being ruined. If recusants were prepared to accept conviction and a moderate fine, they were given letters of protection against all other molestations for their Catholicism.[56]

Compositions enforced by the Northern Commission under Charles I are discussed by:

• Pogson, Fiona. 'Wentworth and the Northern Recusancy
  Commission', *Recusant history* 24(3), 1999, p.271-87.

Not many records of compounding survive. However, those that do are of considerable value. For example, an entry in the Northern Book of Compositions[57] records:

> 17 Sept 1629. Thomas Mennell of Kilvington in the county of York Esq hath by Leonard Brackenburie gent compounded for himselfe Mary his wife, Anthony Mennell his son and Mary his wife for their lands in Thornton le Street And for his Mannor of Northkilinton ….

Papers relating to compositions, together with other recusancy papers, were frequently carefully preserved by the families concerned, and sometimes even bound.[58]

During the Civil War and Interregnum, the task of compounding with Roman Catholics fell to the Parliamentary Committee for Compounding with Delinquents. It was primarily concerned with royalist 'delinquents', but also dealt with Roman Catholics, who were mulcted more heavily than others. In 1649, their compositions were set at one-half of their estates, whereas other royalists paid one-third or one-quarter. The Committee followed much the same procedures as the Northern Commission. Some of its victims were described as 'recusant though not convict' – they had evidently escaped conviction at Quarter Sessions, but were nevertheless pursued by the Committee.[59] The Committee's papers include much genealogical information, as well as details of estates and tenants, and of the involvement of 'delinquents' in the Civil War. They are held among the State Papers in class SP 23.[60] They are sometimes referred to as the Royalist Composition Papers, and are partially calendared in:

• Green, Mary Anne Everett, ed. *Calendar of the Committee for Compounding with Delinquents, &c., 1643-1660.* 5 vols. HMSO, 1889-92. The original records have been microfilmed as part of *The Complete State Papers Domestic.* Numerous microfilm reels + booklet. Harvester Press, 1977.

Certificates of recusants' estates for 1656 can also be found in class C 203/4 (duplicated in SP23/261). Reference may also be made to *A catalogue of the lords, knights, and gentlemen that have compounded for their estates* (1655), available online at **archive.org**.

For a useful guide to the confiscation of lands during the Civil War, see:

• Crown, church and royalist lands 1642-1660
www.nationalarchives.gov.uk/help-with-your-research/research-guides/crown-church-royalist-lands-1642-1660

F. THE EXCHEQUER 2: OTHER RECORDS[61]
Exannual Rolls
The penalties recorded in the Pipe and recusant rolls were not always easy to collect, and could be many years in arrears. Arrearages were transferred to the exannual rolls, class E 363. For the period 1580–1635,

an exannual roll (E 363/9) was devoted solely to recusants' desperate debts. Not all proved to be uncollectable; many entries record that debts had been settled or part-settled.

Memoranda Rolls

As has already been noted, the recusant rolls sometimes refer to authorizations for the seizure of recusants' lands, which are noted on the Memoranda Rolls. There are two series of Memoranda Rolls. Class E 159 were compiled by the King's (or Queen's) Remembrancer. Class E 368 belonged to the Lord Treasurer. These Rolls are dated by regnal year, unlike the recusant rolls. The different systems of dating must be taken into account when comparing entries on them with those in the recusant rolls.

These rolls have a much wider scope than just recusancy. However, their recusant content can be very informative. In addition to the authorization of seizures, they may also record settlements, the discharge of recusants, the release of their property and the evidence on which judgement was entered for the plaintiff.[62] The majority of cross references from the recusant rolls relate to class E368.

The memoranda rolls have been little used, but are of considerable value to the biographer. That value is demonstrated by:

• Bowler, Hugh. 'Exchequer Dossiers: The Recusancy of Venerable John Talbot, Gentleman (1)', *Biographical Studies* 2(1), 1953, p. 4-22.
• Bowler, Hugh. 'Exchequer Dossiers: 2 the Recusancy of Venerable John Bretton, Gentleman and of Frances, His Wife,' *Biographical Studies* 2(2), 1953, p.111-134.

The names of recusancy convicts, 1590 to 1620, who sued for pardon and discharge of their recusancy debts, and are identified by the Memoranda Rolls, are listed by:

• Questier, Michael. 'Sources for Conformity in Elizabethan and Jacobean England', *Catholic Ancestor* 5(5), 1995, p.187-92; 5(6), 1995, p.240-5; 6(1), 1996, p.11-14; 6(2), 1996, p.57-65; 6(3), 1996, p.95-100. Note that successive issues have slightly different titles, and cover a different region.

Pells of Receipt

The Clerk of the Pells recorded all monies paid into or out of the Exchequer. Receipt rolls and books are in the National Archives, class E 401. These too are dated by regnal years. Until the reign of Charles I, they record the names of recusants who paid their fines, and are much easier to search than the recusant rolls. Thereafter, although they continue to record receipts, they do not give recusants' names.

Treasury Books

Many papers relating to recusancy can be identified in the *Calendar of Treasury Books* (32 vols. HMSO, 1904-57), which cover 1660–1718, and the *Calendar of Treasury Books and Papers* (5 vols. HMSO, 1897-1903), which cover 1729–1745. These yield much information on individual Catholics.

Miscellaneous Exchequer Documents

A number of other Exchequer documents concern recusancy and Catholicism. Summonses for recusancy, 1558–1625, together with notes on arrears, are in E 389. Sheriffs' accounts of seizures prior to 1660 are in E 379. Accounts of revenue from recusants' forfeitures can be found in a variety of classes:

- E 101. King's Remembrancer Accounts[63], including rentals, accounts, and other documents relating to recusant estates.
- E 178. Special Commissions of Inquiry into matters such as priests, recusants, and forfeitures, 16-17th c.
- E 351/408-52. Pipe Office Declared Accounts, including fines for offences against penal statutes, 1557-1684.

For accounts and other documents from related departments, see:

- AO 1. Accounts of the Receiver of Revenue from Popish Recusants, c.1627-55
- AO 3/366/1-3. Forfeitures: Accounts of Revenues from Recusants, 1635-9,
- LR 7/87 Receiver's Declarations of Recusant Forfeitures, c.1630-57.

Exchequer litigation records may also provide useful information. Bills and answers in E 112, the Barons' depositions in E 133, depositions taken by commission in E 134, and the decrees and orders of the Court in E 123–31,[64] all provide information regarding disputed title to recusants' estates on which leases had been granted by the Crown.

Records of disbursements may also have Catholic interest. The cost of arresting and gaoling prisoners had to be met; prisoners had to be conveyed from place to place; witnesses had to be recompensed. For Tower Bills, sent in by the Lieutenant of the Tower between 1575 and 1681, and listing his expenses in accommodating Roman Catholic prisoners, see:

- Pollen, J.H., ed. 'Tower Bills', *Miscellanea 3*. Catholic Record Society, 3. 1906, p.4-29; *Miscellanea 4*. Catholic Record Society 4. 1907, p.223-46.

G. REGISTRATIONS OF PAPISTS ESTATES

The Act of 1715 mentioned above required Papists to register their estates with the Clerk of the Peace. These registrations can be found among Quarter Sessions records. Clerks of the Peace reported them to the Commissioners for Forfeited Estates (see below, p.96–8), whose registrations can be found in class FEC 1/1113-1314. A further registration act was passed in 1722; 450 returns made under it to the Exchequer are in class E 174/1. There were various subsequent acts, and registration continued until the Catholic Relief Act 1791. Estates are described in some detail, including precise locations and acreages, with topographical and building details. Tenants are named, with details of tenure, and rents may be given. It is not always clear whether the names returned were Catholics or non-jurors. A number of registrations have been published. Returns made to the Forfeited Estates Commissioners in 1715 are summarised in:

- Estcourt, Edgar E., & Payne, John Orlebar, eds. *The English Catholic nonjurors of 1715, being a Summary of the Register of their Estates*. Burns & Oates, [1885][65].

Durham
- Hudleston, C.Roy, ed. *Durham Recusants Estates 1717-1778*. Surtees Society, 173. 1962. Continued in *Miscellanea 3*. Surtees Society, 175. 1965.

- Fewster, Elizabeth. 'The Valuation of Catholic Estates in Durham, 1724', Northern Catholic History 30, 1989, p.17-28; 31, 1990, p.26-37.

Kent
- Hart, W.H. *A Register of the Lands held by Catholics and Nonjurors in the County of Kent in the Reign of King George I.* J Russell Smith, 1870. Reprinted British Library, 2011.

Lancashire
- France, R. Sharpe, ed. *The Registers of Estates of Lancashire Papists, 1717-1788.* 3 vols. Lancashire & Cheshire Record Society, 98, 108, & 117. 1945-77. Vol.1. 1717. Vol.2. 1717. Vol.3. 1717, with lists of persons registered, 1718-1775.

Northumberland
- Hodgson, J.C., ed. *Northumbrian Documents of the Seventeenth and Eighteenth Centuries, comprising the register of the estates of Roman Catholic in Northumberland, and the correspondence of Miles Stapylton.* Surtees Society 131. 1918.

Yorkshire
- 'Registration of Papists Estates', in Atkinson, J.C., ed. *Quarter Sessions Records.* North Riding Record Society, 7. 1889, p.251-91, & 8, 1890, p.1-136.

H. FORFEITED ESTATES COMMISSION
The Forfeited Estates Commission was established to deal with estates forfeited for treason in the 1715 Jacobite Rebellion. Many Roman Catholics were implicated in the rebellion, and the Commissioners' records include various lists of Papists. For example, FEC 2/125 seems to be a nationwide list of recusants convicted before the rebellion, and perhaps compiled in order to assist the Commission's work.

Commissioners had to identify estates, receive their rents and sell them. They were assisted by Quarter Sessions' registration of recusant estates discussed above. The minute books of the Commissioners are held by the National Archives, class FEC 2. They are accompanied by registers of claims against estates, decree books, registers of appeals, letters and petitions.

The Commissioners seized the deeds of forfeited estates, and accumulated a large collection. Some of these date back to the sixteenth century and earlier. These are in FEC 1, mostly arranged by the names of those attainted. Registers of these estates, arranged by county, are in FEC 1/1113-1323. For a detailed guide to the records of the Commission, see:

• Barlow, D. *The records of the Forfeited Estates Commission.* Public Record Office handbooks 12. HMSO, 1968.

For a listing of all the names mentioned in FEC 1, see:

• Jolly, Emma. 'Jacobite material: the records of the Forfeited Estates Commission for England', *Genealogists' magazine* 28(11), 2006, p.493-8.

Other sources for Jacobite rebels are identified by:

• How to Look for Records of Jacobite Risings 1715 & 1745 **www.nationalarchives.gov.uk/help-with-your-research/ research-guides/jacobite-risings-1715-and-1745.**
• Scott, Geoffrey. 'English Catholicism and the archives of the Jacobite movement', *Catholic Archives* 35, 2015, p.66-76.

A chapter on the history of the Forfeited Estates Commission is included in a general account of the fate of Jacobite prisoners:

• Sankey, Margaret. *Jacobite Prisoners of the 1715 Rebellion: Preventing and Punishing Insurrection in Early Hanoverian Britain.* Ashgate, 2005.

Superstitious Uses
Throughout the penal period, property given to 'superstitious uses' was liable to seizure. Consequently, Catholic institutions could not own property themselves, and had to rely on laymen to act as trustees for the property they used. For example, throughout the eighteenth century the Hussey family of Marnhull (Dorset) acted as trustees for the Benedictine house in Bath.[66]

The Forfeited Estates Commission interested itself in such property. FEC 1/779 identifies houses in which mass had been said. Depositions regarding superstitious uses are in FEC 1/1527-9.

'Superstitious uses' were also the subject of inquiry by other government departments. A number of Chancery reports are in C 205/19. Interrogatories and depositions in an Exchequer case relating to 'superstitious uses' are printed in:

• Burton, Edwin Hubert, ed. 'Official documents relating to an enquiry as to the estate of Robert Charnock of Leyland, priest, left for 'superstitious uses' 1687', *Miscellanea* 10. Catholic Record Society 17. 1915, p.327-62.

For the 1690s, see:

• Hopkins, P.A. 'The Commission into Superstitious Lands of the 1690s', *Recusant History* 15(4), 1980, p.265-82.

I. TAX LISTS

The government was not above imposing additional levies on Catholics, even after they had been heavily fined. During the 1580s, a levy of horses was imposed on wealthier recusants on at least three occasions. A number of documents in the State Papers give details of these levies: SP 12/142/33, SP 12/183/15 and SP 12/200/61.[67] On each occasion, fewer than 300 recusants paid; however, some of these levies were based on a census of 1582 (SP 12/156/42), which reported 1,939 convicted recusants.

A further levy of horse was made in 1598. Again, the government was able to collect a fairly voluminous amount of information concerning the wealth of Catholics, although no summary listing of taxpayers survive.[68]

In the seventeenth century, the subsidy was the major Parliamentary tax. From 1628, convicted recusants were required to pay double, and are identified as recusants in the resultant assessments. Those not liable to pay subsidies were nevertheless subjected to a poll tax, which was recorded on the subsidy rolls. This poll tax had a wider incidence. It applied not only to recusants, but also to non-communicants. The rolls can be used for statistical purposes; in Carolinian Lancashire, for example, they list 2,230 recusants in West Darby Hundred, and 860 in Amounderness Hundred.[69] Over 600 recusants have been identified in the subsidy rolls for the Barony of Kendal during Charles I's reign.[70]

Recusants also had to pay double when assessed to certain other direct taxes; for example, the graduated poll tax of 1641, and the grant of £400,000 made in 1642. Subsidies were replaced by the hearth tax in 1662, and double payment ceased. Subsidy assessments are now held by the National Archives, class E 179. See:

- E 179 Database
  www.nationalarchives.gov.uk/e179

Stray records can also be found in local record offices. Many returns have been published by county record societies.

Double taxation was re-imposed when the land tax was introduced in 1692. This supplanted the levying of recusancy fines and forfeitures; the recusant rolls ceased in 1691. Tax assessments list, year by year, the names of landowners and occupiers in each parish. Recusants are identified in assessments, except where they successfully evaded payment. Liability was sometimes attached to land owned by Catholics, rather than to Catholics themselves; anyone who purchased land owned by a recusant had to pay double, regardless of whether they were Catholic or not. Liability for payment was sometimes passed on to tenants; Lord Shrewsbury, for one, wrote this requirement into his Staffordshire tenants' leases. Catholics remained liable to double taxation until 1794, although it was sporadically exacted until 1831; costs involved in reducing liability tended to be greater than accepting liability. Each county paid a fixed amount, which was unaffected by changes in the law relating to recusants. Any alteration in the amount paid by one taxpayer had to be made up by other taxpayers.

Survival of land tax assessments are patchy; the great majority post-date around 1780. They are generally found in local record offices. Receivers' accounts in E 181 (arranged by county) record the names of those who paid double, but are not complete. The particulars of accounts of land and assessed taxes in E 182 do not usually give names. A few certificates of the Land Tax Commissioners concerning the assessment of double tax can be found in the National Archives, class E 174. The National Archives also holds an almost complete set of land tax returns for 1798, in class IR 23. This class also contains papers relating to the appeals of Roman Catholics against double assessment (IR 23/122-6).

Useful discussions of the double land tax are provided by:

- Williams, J. Anthony. 'An Unexamined Aspect of the Penal Laws: the Problem of the Double Land-Tax', *Dublin Review*, Spring 1959, p.32-7.
- Rowlands, Marie. 'The Iron Age of Double Taxation', *Staffordshire Catholic History* 3, 1963, p.30-46.

For a listing of surviving land tax returns, see:

- Gibson, J.S.W., & Medlycott, M., & Mills, D. *Land and window tax assessments.* Federation of Family History Societies, 1993.

Another tax specifically on recusants was imposed in 1723, in the wake of the Atterbury Plot. This levy, amounting to £100,000, was assessed on the basis of the 1715 registers discussed above (see p.95–6). Some information concerning this tax is in class E 182. There are also accounts in E 369/125.

J. IMPRISONMENT

Penalties for Catholicism could be much worse than mere fines and forfeitures. Some were executed, many were imprisoned. Catholic priests used imprisonment to good purpose; many prisons, especially in London, became Catholic community centres, through which both Catholic prisoners and their numerous visitors passed. They acted as information centres, and places from which Catholic books could be distributed. Indeed, some effectively became mass centres.

Many lists of Catholic prisoners can be found among the State Papers, Quarter Sessions records and various other sources. For a printed listing of Elizabethan prisoners, see:

- Pollen, J.H., ed. 'Official lists of Prisoners for Religion during the Reign of Queen Elizabeth', in *Miscellanea 1*. Catholic Record Society, 1. 1905, p.47-72; *Miscellanea 2*. Catholic Record Society 2, 1906, p.219-88.

K. OATHS

Roman Catholics were required to take various oaths, although many refused to do so. Such refusal was liable to be certified to the Justices at Quarter Sessions, and refusers are likely to be mentioned in presentments, indictments, order books and other records.

When the Civil War was about to break out, the House of Commons ordered the taking of the Protestation 'against all Popery and Popish innovations'. Obviously, many Roman Catholics – although not all – refused the oath.[71] One of the aims of the order was to identify them, and they may therefore be listed in returns, which are available online. See:

• Protestation Returns
www.parliament.uk/business/publications/parliamentary-archives/explore-guides-to-documentary-archive-/family history/sources/protestations

See also:

• Gibson, Jeremy, & Dell, Alan. *The protestation returns and other contemporary listings*. Federation of Family History Societies, 1995 (2004 reprint).

Those who refused to swear the oath of allegiance after 1714 are listed by county in C 203/6, and by Estcourt and Payne (above, p.95). For those who refused the oath in Lancashire in 1715, see class KB 18. Worcestershire refusers are listed in:

• English, W.E. 'Worcestershire nonjurors in 1715', *Midland Catholic History* 4, 1995, p.23-38.

For the West Riding, see:

• West Yorkshire Roman Catholic Oath Records, 1714-1787, 1829
http://search.ancestry.co.uk/search/db.aspx?dbid=8632
This collection also includes an 1829 register of Roman Catholic priests.

Not everyone asked to take these oaths refused to do so. Returns of those who took the oaths of supremacy and allegiance in the metropolis in 1678 are held by the Parliamentary Archives.[72] After the passage of the Catholic Relief Acts of 1778 and 1791, oaths of loyalty acceptable to Catholics were required. A number of lists of oath-takers have been published; see:

- Worrall, Edw. S. 'The Essex register of Oaths Subscribed under the Catholic Relief Act 1778', *Essex Recusant* 6(1), 1964, p.17-27.
- Worrall, Edw. S. 'The Essex register of Oaths Subscribed under the Catholic Relief Act 1791', *Essex Recusant* 6(2), 1964, p.57-65.
- Rhodes, Murray. 'Worcestershire Oath Takers, 1791-3', *Midland Catholic History* 6, 1998, p.39-45.

Many oath rolls can be found among Quarter Sessions records, and in the National Archive, classes E 169 and CP 37. The 1778 Act permitted Catholic attorneys to practise in the central courts. They had to take a special oath; records are in CP 37/1, CP 10/18-20, E 3/4 and C 217/180/5. Oaths of Roman Catholic solicitors 1838–1867 are in C 214/23/1. The Sacramental Test Act 1828 ended the requirement for office holders to take the sacrament, and substituted an oath which Catholics could take. The Roman Catholic Emancipation Act 1829 removed other objectionable clauses from oaths required from Roman Catholics. Rolls recording oaths taken by Roman Catholics subsequent to these acts are in the National Archives, C 214/21 and C 214/23/2.

L. MEETING HOUSE LICENCES

The act of 1791 extended the registration of dissenters' meeting house to Roman Catholic chapels and schools. Registration had to be made by Clerks of the Peace. In 1852, their registers were replaced by the Worship Register, kept by the Registrar General. He obtained returns of all former registrations of both Roman Catholic chapels, and Nonconformist meeting houses. These are in class RG31. Certificates sent in to register chapels after 1851 are in RG70. The ongoing Worship Register is described in:

- Rose, R.B. 'Some national sources for protestant Nonconformist and Roman Catholic history', *Bulletin of the Institute of Historical Research* 31, 1958, p.79-83.

For a list of buildings registered, see:

• *Return of churches, chapels, and buildings registered for religious worship in the registration districts of Great Britain, showing the religious denomination to which such churches, chapels and buildings belong.* Parliamentary papers series, 1882.

M. STATE PAPERS
The State Papers (SP classes), briefly mentioned above, are the papers of the Secretaries of State from 1547 until 1782. They cover an extraordinarily wide range of topics, and include a massive amount of information on Roman Catholicism. Some examples of relevant documents include:

• SP 12/243/80, f.221r-222v. Intercepted letter from Cardinal Allen.
• SP 12/152/3. List of Catholics whose children had been sent overseas for their education, 1582.
• SP 14/216. Papers related to Gunpowder Plot.[73]
• SP 16/99. Details of the discovery of a Jesuit college at Clerkenwell, 1628.
• SP 20/8. Decisions on appeals against sequestration lodged by Catholics, c.1649-50.
• SP 34/26. Returns of Papists, 1708.
• SP 37/20/21. Papers concerning the Gordon Riots, 1780.

The original State Papers Domestic have been microfilmed for the period 1547–1702, and are available in many research libraries:

• *The Complete State Papers Domestic.* Harvester Press, 1977.

They are also available online (through institutions):

• State Papers Online 1509–1714
http://gale.cengage.co.uk/state-papers-online-15091714.aspx

There are also extensive printed *Calendars of State Papers* (up to 1704) and *Calendars of Home Office papers* (for 1760-75), many of which are available online at British History Online **www.british-history.ac.uk/ catalogue/guides-and-calendars**. The editing of these calendars varied in depth, and they should be regarded as guides to the records rather than substitutes for them. Various supplementary calendars have been issued by the List and Index Society **http://royalhistsoc.org/ publications/national-history-and-record-societies** (click name), which has also issued calendars for the reign of George I.

For a detailed guide to the Catholic content of the state papers, see Chapter 5 of Williams' *Sources for Recusant history* (see above, p.XXX). See also:

• Home affairs in the Early Modern Period: State Papers Domestic 1547–1649
www.nationalarchives.gov.uk/help-with-your-research/ research-guides/state-papers-domestic-1547-1649
Similar guides cover the periods 1642–60, 1660–1714, and 1714–82.

The state papers include the records of the Civil War Committees for Compounding with Delinquents, and for Advance of Money. The former has already been discussed. The Committee for Advance of Money was responsible for raising loans 'on the public faith'. Its proceedings (in class SP 143) contain many references to Catholics, and have been partially calendared by:

• Green, Mary Anne Everett, ed. *Calendar of the proceedings of the Committee for Advance of Money, 1642-1656.* 3 vols. HMSO, 1888.

In addition to the State Papers Domestic, there are many references to Catholics in the State Papers (Foreign). A guide to these papers, and to the printed calendars, is provided by:

• How to Look for State Papers Foreign 1509–1782
www.nationalarchives.gov.uk/help-with-your-research/ research-guides/state-papers-foreign-1509-1782

The State Papers also include the Commonwealth Exchequer Papers (SP 28). These are the financial records of the Parliamentary and Interregnum governments, including warrants, accounts, minutes, committee papers, and a variety of other documents. They include much information relating to recusants. For example, SP 28/217 consists of inventories of the goods of 'Papists and Delinquents', itemising their furniture, their livestock and their farming implements in great detail.

These papers also include some records of the Parliamentary county committees,[74] which governed the counties for Parliament during the Civil War and Interregnum. Their minutes provide much information regarding Catholic 'delinquents' and their property. For example, the Staffordshire Committee (the minutes of which are at the William Salt Library, Stafford) noted that Thomas Underhill the younger of Bishbery, a recusant, had paid his composition, and ordered 'that his beasts shall be delivered unto him and that his person and estate shall be protected'.[75]

Many papers which ought to be among the State Papers have strayed, and are now to be found in other repositories, especially the British Library (see p.44–5). For example, the Library's Add MS 34011-34017 are returns of suspected persons made by the Cromwellian Major Generals in 1655. Many 'strays' are held among the private papers of former government officials, such as Lord Burghley and Sir Julius Caesar; for these, see below, p.187–8.

N. PRIVY COUNCIL PAPERS

Recusancy was regularly discussed by the Privy Council. A wide range of papers, such as letters, rolls, books, files and printed material came to its attention, and are now in the National Archives. PC 1 contains miscellaneous papers dating from around 1680. PC 1/13, f.73, for example, lists the proclamations concerning Catholics made between 1690 and 1743. PC 1/2, f.41 is a copy of the letter sent to the Archbishops in 1706 ordering them to conduct a census of Catholics. Roman Catholics who took an oath in 1796 are listed in PC 1/37/107.

The registers of the Privy Council, dating from 1540, are in PC 2. They record the decisions made by the Council, and the directives it issued. The registers give much information regarding recusants. The Council interrogated those who were brought before it, and perhaps imprisoned them, or bound them to good behaviour. The 9th Lord Stourton, for example, was arrested when, as a young man in 1573, he tried to flee to the Continent. He was placed in the custody of the Archbishop of Canterbury so that he could be 'better instructed'; he was subsequently bound to 'good behaviour', and forbidden to leave the realm without licence.[76] Numerous licences to travel, both within the realm and overseas, are mentioned in Privy Council registers. In 1627, Lady Anne Brett, a convicted recusant, was licensed 'to travel out of the compass of her confinement, she being diseased, to recover her health; to come up to London and Westminster, and to goe into the countyes of Devon, Somerset and Wilts., etc., for the term of six moneths'.[77]

The Council was also interested in the revenue to be obtained from recusant fines and forfeitures. Occasionally, such revenue was granted to courtiers and others, rather than passing through the Exchequer process. Records of such grants can be found in the Patent Rolls, and also in the Privy Council registers. In 1580, for example, Nicholas Anesley held letters patent granting him certain fines and forfeitures in Lancashire; registers record that the Council had to intervene in order to ensure that he obtained the revenues he was entitled to by the grant.[78] Details of such 'privatised' fines and forfeitures would not be recorded in the recusant rolls or other Exchequer records.

Many Privy Council registers are in print:

- Dasent, J.R., et al, eds. *Acts of the Privy Council of England, 1542-1631.* 46 vols. H.M.S.O., 1890-1964. View online via British History Online **www.british-history.ac.uk**.
- *Privy Council registers preserved in the Public Record Office reproduced in facsimile: 1 June, 1637-[August, 1645].* 12 vols. HMSO, 1967-1968.

Class PC 4 consists of bound minutes of the Privy Council's proceedings, 1670–1795, continued by indexed entry books from 1795. Not everything in these minutes has an entry in the register.

For other Privy Council records, see:

- How to look for Records of Privy Council since 1386 **www.nationalarchives.gov.uk/help-with-your-research/ research-guides/privy-council-since-1386**

O. CHANCERY RECORDS

A wide variety of administrative and judicial records from the Court of Chancery, some of which have already been mentioned, relate to Roman Catholics. The Patent Rolls and the Close Rolls are both important general historical sources, and offer much information on recusancy.

Patent Rolls

Royal grants of land, offices, pensions, pardons and licences were made by letters patent, and enrolled on the Patent Rolls in Chancery (C 66). After 1558, many relate to Catholics; for example, grants of forfeited lands, pardons for convicted recusants and licences to travel overseas. There are many commissions to take action against recusants, and especially against Jesuits, to lease recusants' properties and to tender oaths.

Patent Rolls have printed calendars prior to 1601; for details, see the guide mentioned below. For the succeeding period, the original indexes to the rolls in C 274 are available; those for James I's reign have been published by the List and Index Society. The letters patent themselves can frequently be found among family and local archives. Much supplementary material can be found among the State Papers and in other sources.

It may sometimes be easier to search related Chancery series than the post-1601 rolls. From 1595, commissions can be identified in the Crown Office Docket Books (C 231 and, from 1617, C 233), and in Chancery Miscellaneous Books (C 193). Petitions for grants and commissions until 1645 are among the King's Bills in the Signet Office (SO 3).[79] For grants made after 1660, see the *Calendar of Treasury Books* (see above, p.94). The British Library also holds relevant material. A particularly useful volume is provided by Additional Manuscript 34765, which extensively lists grants relating to recusants made by letters patent, 1606–1611. For more information, see:

• Royal grants in letters patent and charters from 1199
  **www.nationalarchives.gov.uk/help-with-your-research/
  research-guides/royal-grants-letters-patent-charters-from-1199**

Close Rolls

Under a statute of 1716–17, recusant wills and deeds had to be enrolled. The Close Rolls (C 54) were used for this purpose. For wills, see below, p.193. After the Catholic Relief Act 1791, Roman Catholics began to emulate Nonconformists by enrolling their chapel deeds on the Close rolls.

Chapter 5

BIRTHS, MARRIAGES AND DEATHS

Family historians need to know the dates of their ancestors' births, marriages and deaths. This information is also very useful to local historians. Prior to the advent of civil registration, we must normally rely on dates of baptisms and burials, rather than on dates of births and deaths. Mostly, baptisms took place within a few days of birth, and burials within a few days of death. In England, these dates have been recorded in Church of England parish registers since 1538. Similar registers were not kept by Roman Catholics for almost another two centuries, since, had they been discovered, they could have placed those named in them in danger of prosecution.[1]

A ANGLICAN PARISH REGISTERS

Church of England parish registers of baptisms, marriages and burials were first introduced by Henry VIII's vicegerent, Thomas Cromwell – probably as a result of the fact that he had seen similar registers being kept in Roman Catholic countries on the Continent during his youthful travels. Cromwell's injunction to keep registers remained in force during the reigns of all the later Tudor monarchs, both Protestant and Catholic. Under Mary, Cardinal Pole ordered that baptismal entries should include the names of godparents, as well as the names of parents and child. They stood in a spiritual relationship with the baptised, and canon law prohibited godparents marrying their godchildren. Very few Marian registers now survive, as the old paper registers had to be copied into parchment at the end of Elizabeth's reign. Most copyists only copied the names of parents and children, not the names of godparents.[2]

It took several decades for worshippers to realise that there would be no going back to Roman Catholicism. Consequently, many of those unwilling to turn Protestant nevertheless continued to celebrate baptisms, marriages and burials in their parish churches. However, when the realisation dawned that the Roman Catholic hierarchy were unwilling to countenance continuation of this practice, Papists gradually withdrew from their parish churches and celebrated their own vital events. Marian priests could legally celebrate marriages.[3] It was only after around 1590 that the ecclesiastical courts started to prosecute marriages conducted by Catholic priests. Prosecutions in these courts were discussed in Chapter 4.

There was considerable pressure on Catholics to participate in Anglican rites. This pressure stemmed primarily from two sources. One of the justifications Cromwell had used for the introduction of parish registers had been that they would enable inheritance rights to be proved. For Catholic landowners, this was important. If they were unable to ensure that appropriate entries were made in parish registers, their claims to inheritance could be disputed.

An Act of 1606, passed in the wake of Gunpowder Plot, emphasised the importance of register entries for proving the right to inheritance. It required Catholics to have their babies baptised by an Anglican priest, and their dead buried in the parish churchyard. The penalty for evasion was a fine of £100 for a baptism and £20 for a burial. Husbands could lose their right to their wives' property, and wives could lose their dower.[4] The Act justified itself by stating:

> And for that popish recusants are not usually married nor their children christened nor themselves buried, according to the laws of the Church of England, but the same are done superstitiously by popish persons in secret, whereby the days of their marriage, birth and burial cannot be certainly known...[5]

The Act does not seem to have had a great impact on Catholic practice. However, these considerations prompted some Catholics to find ways of ensuring that appropriate entries were made in parish registers. It was possible to make the plea that a child's life had been in danger, and that consequently a midwife or someone else had been compelled to baptise the child before the parish priest could attend. Such baptisms were common, and might be entered in parish registers as private baptisms. Alternatively, the child could be baptised by both a Catholic priest and the Anglican incumbent. The Catholic hierarchy also permitted parents to pay the incumbent to enter the baptism in the register. In the eighteenth century, the fact that babies had been baptised by Roman Catholic priests was sometimes entered in Anglican registers.

The range of possibilities may be illustrated by the register of Stourton (Wiltshire).[6] The Barnes family were prominent Catholics in the parish, and were numerous. However, there is no baptismal entry in the parish register between 1629 and 1703. On 3 May 1703, the baptism of Walter, the son of Walter and Elizabeth Barnes, is entered. The entry was, however, interlined, and written by a different hand from that of the other entries in that year. The entry was omitted in the bishop's transcript, which had to be sent to the bishop annually. The entry for the baptism of the same couple's son Robert, on 3 September 1704, was similarly interlined. The bishop's transcript does not give the date, but it does record that Robert and two other babies were 'baptised by popish priest'. It is not clear who made the interlineation, or, indeed, who wrote the original register. Legally, that was the duty of the rector, although the task was frequently performed by the parish clerk, churchwardens or a paid scribe. Someone evidently decided that the baptisms of a leading family in the parish ought to be registered. Or perhaps Walter Barnes senior himself put pressure on someone to do so.

Many other parish registers mention Roman Catholic births and baptisms. At Pyrton (Oxfordshire) in 1635 the vicar recorded baptisms of children that he had entered 'at the request of Mr Shepherd, Mr William Stonor's curate', that is, his Roman Catholic priest.[7] The vicar of Stock (Essex) listed 'children... born in Stock parish but not baptised by ye minister their parents being papists'.[8] Sometimes, the word 'born' rather than 'baptised' provides the only indication that children were the offspring of Catholics or dissenters. The vicar of Warblington (Hampshire) recorded the baptism of Thomas Ring 'by a Romish priest' in 1698, but in 1710 he simply wrote that William Todd was 'born'.[9]

Some of these entries were influenced by legislation of 1694 and 1695, which imposed a tax on baptisms, marriages and burials, and which required incumbents to expand the scope of their registers to include Nonconformist and Roman Catholic ceremonies as well as those conducted under the auspices of the Church of England. At Hampstead

Norris (Berkshire), the incumbent kept *A register of ye Persons married buried Chrystened or born among ye papists Quakers and such like in the parish of Hampstead Norris since May 1st 1695.*[10] Such registers were widely kept, at least in the North East. It is possible that some Roman Catholic children were registered as illegitimate: their parents had not been legally married by a Church of England clergyman.

Not all Anglican priests bothered to register Roman Catholic children. Probably, the majority did not. Wardour (Wiltshire), which lay in the Anglican parish of Tisbury, was the most important centre of Catholicism in Wiltshire. A comparison of Wardour's Catholic baptismal register with the Anglican parish register of Tisbury reveals that there were 600 entries in the former between 1744 and 1791, none of which were mentioned in the Tisbury register.[11]

Roman Catholic marriages are recorded much less frequently than baptisms in parish registers.[12] The Roman Catholic hierarchy strongly discouraged marriages in Anglican parish churches. Nevertheless, some Catholics underwent two ceremonies – one publicly in the parish church, then one in secret before a Roman Catholic priest. The secret marriage would not be acknowledged in the parish register. The public Anglican ceremony would safeguard the inheritance of any children, and prevent possible prosecution for fornication. The gentry frequently obtained a marriage licence, rather than having banns called. Consequently, it may be worthwhile to check marriage licence records.[13]

During the Interregnum, between 1653 and 1660, marriage law underwent a revolution. Marriage became a civil ceremony, conducted by a Justice of the Peace rather than a clergyman. Entries continued to be made in parish registers, but not by a clergyman. Instead a lay official, confusingly known as a 'parish register', had to be appointed by parishioners in each parish. Roman Catholics generally accepted this procedure, and consequently this is the only period before emancipation when most of their marriages are recorded in parish registers (although they may also have undergone a ceremony before a Roman Catholic priest).[14] After the Restoration, the law reverted to the old status quo.

Until 1753, marriage was the subject of conflict between the common law and canon law. The former recognised any marriage that had been conducted before witnesses. The latter specified that marriage had to take place at the church door, and to be conducted by an

Anglican priest. A Catholic marriage was therefore valid under common law, despite the fact that the parties could be accused of clandestine marriage before the courts of the established church. This conflict of laws was ended by Lord Hardwicke's 1753 Marriage Act.

Hardwicke's Act was not primarily aimed at Catholics. Rather, its purpose was to abolish common law marriage, and thus to prevent clandestine marriages taking place in the Fleet Prison and other centres. The large numbers of clandestine marriages conducted by clergymen who had no episcopal supervision had become a great scandal. After the Act, valid marriages could only be conducted by Church of England clergymen, unless the parties were Quakers or Jews. Attempts to secure exemption for Catholics from the requirement proved unsuccessful.

Catholics were divided in their reaction. Some, including Bishop Challoner, preferred Catholics to flout the law completely. Attendance at an Anglican service was seen as denial of the faith. However, Challoner recognised that the ceremony might have to be gone through out of sheer necessity. He recommended that it be treated as a civil ceremony, that the couple should refuse to kneel or pray, and that a Roman Catholic priest should also conduct a marriage ceremony.[15] It was not clear whether that should be before or after the Anglican ceremony. Despite the fact that the Anglican ceremony lacked religious legitimacy in Catholic eyes, Catholics did regard it as legally binding; some thought it made a second Catholic ceremony redundant. If the Catholic ceremony took place before the Anglican ceremony, that would be a clandestine marriage in the eyes of the law, and would render both the parties and the priest liable to the penalty of transportation. In practice, most Catholics were married first in the parish church, and secondly by one of their own priests.[16]

Hardwicke's Act made an important change in the way in which Anglican marriage registers were written. Hitherto, there had been no consistency in the information recorded. In some registers, only the names of the parties were recorded. In others, entries were much more detailed. Henceforth, entries had to be made in books of printed forms. The Act specified the details required: the names and parishes of the parties, the date and place of marriage, whether by banns or licence, whether with the consent of parents or guardians, the name of the officiating minister and the signatures of the parties, witnesses and minister. These requirements remained in force until the advent of civil registration in 1837, when the prohibition on Catholic marriages ended.

There was, of course, agitation against the illegality of Catholic marriage. In 1823, the parish officers of St Luke, Old Street, Middlesex, drew attention to the fact that many Irish Catholics in their parish were married by Catholic priests, and did not legalise their marriages by an Anglican ceremony. Their children were legally bastards, chargeable to the parish for poor relief.[17] Such arguments may have carried more weight with Parliament than the case that the Catholics themselves put. They also suggest that genealogists might find much information about Irish Catholics in the records of the poor law.

Catholic burials normally took place in Anglican parish churchyards. There was frequently nowhere else to bury the dead, and burials were recorded in parish registers. Such entries may be noted 'recusant' or 'papist', although that became less common in the eighteenth and nineteenth century. One particularly tolerant Anglican incumbent, recording Bishop Challoner's burial at Milton (Berkshire), recorded: 'Anno Domini 1781 January 22. Buried the Reverend Richard Challoner, a Popish Priest and Titular Bishop of London and Salisbury. A very pious and good man, of great learning and extensive abilities'.[18]

Bishop Richard Challoner.

Roman Catholic burial in Anglican churchyards was not without controversy. The law placed Roman Catholic corpses in a legal limbo. Many Roman Catholics were excommunicated by the Anglican church courts. Excommunicants were not entitled to be buried in consecrated ground, but the Act of 1606 forbade burial anywhere other than in a Protestant cemetery. Sometimes burial was refused, especially in the century after 1558.

Licences to bury excommunicants could be applied for, but were rarely issued. For many Catholics, that did not matter greatly. They wanted their dead buried in consecrated ground (churchyards had mostly been consecrated by priests of their own faith before the Reformation). But they insisted on funeral services conducted by their own priests, and refused the Anglican burial service. Asking permission to bury a corpse was likely to lead to the incumbent insisting on doing so, if he did not refuse permission. Therefore, Catholics were frequently buried secretly in the churchyard at night. A service might be held beforehand in a private house, although sometimes the priest went to the churchyard with the corpse.

Such clandestine burials frequently took place without the knowledge of Anglican incumbents. However, the fact of a death in a parish of a few hundred souls was likely to come to the knowledge of the incumbent, and the evidence of disturbed soil in the churchyard would also be clear. Parish registers sometimes record such burials. For example, a 1642 entry in the North Elmham (Norfolk) parish register reads:

> Rose, the wife of Robert Lunford was buried the 23 of December, she was a recusant papist, she was buried in the night without the church ceremonies.[19]

Those who participated in clandestine burial could be prosecuted. However, such prosecutions were probably few. Indeed, churchwardens, who were supposed to present such activities in the ecclesiastical courts, were sometimes involved themselves. For example, they supplied the coffin and a burial cloth when the recusant John Pickering of Bowbank (Cumberland) was buried in 1678.[20]

Eighteenth-century Anglican incumbents were frequently willing to allow Catholic priests to conduct their own funerals. At Tisbury

(Wiltshire), a separate section of the churchyard was set aside for Roman Catholic burials. No fewer than eight Catholic priests were buried in the churchyard at Marnhull (Dorset) between 1697 and 1828.[21]

In some places, Catholic gentry and aristocracy had their own vaults. That was the case at Stourton (Wiltshire), where the parish register records the burials of successive Lords Stourton, without mentioning that they were Roman Catholics. When, in 1727, the vicar of Broughton (Yorkshire) attempted to bring a case against Stephen Tempest, Esq., for burying his relatives in his vault without permission, the Archbishop pointed out that Tempest had rights in the vault, and that, in any case, by the Act of 1606 he could not bury them elsewhere.[22]

Parish registers occasionally include information that has nothing to do with baptisms, marriages and burials. They were frequently used as commonplace books, where any information concerning the parish could be recorded for posterity. That sometimes included details of Roman Catholic activities. For example, the register of Scotter (Lincolnshire) includes lists of excommunicants. The Kelvedon Hatch (Essex) register identifies those who refused to take the Protestation oath in 1641–42; while in Odstock (Wiltshire) the register mentions the 1767 Catholic census.

The aim of the preceding paragraphs has been to demonstrate the extent to which Roman Catholic entries of baptisms, marriages and burials can be found in Anglican parish registers. A full account of those registers, however, is beyond the scope of this book. A reasonably up-to-date account is provided by:

• Raymond, Stuart A. *Parish Registers: A History and Guide.* Family History Partnership, 2009.

Anglican registers have generally been deposited in local record offices. For a summary listing, see:

• Humphery-Smith, Cecil. *The Phillimore Atlas and Index of Parish Registers.* (3rd ed. Phillimore, 2003).

More detailed listings are provided in the county volumes of the Society of Genealogists' *National index of parish registers.* These also include listings of Roman Catholic registers.

Many parish registers are available online on sites such as Family Search **http://familysearch.org**, as well as on commercial sites such as Ancestry **www.ancestry.co.uk**, The Genealogist **www.thegenealogist. co.uk** and Find My Past **www.findmypast. co.uk**. Some of these sites include extensive indexes; for example, Boyd's marriage index (1538–1840) is available at both Find My Past and at Genes Reunited **www.genesreunited.co.uk**. The International Genealogical Index (which includes coverage of some Roman Catholic registers) is on the Family Search site.

The Civil Registration Act 1836 ended the practice of entering Roman Catholic vital events in Anglican parish registers. It did not, however, end the practice of keeping Roman Catholic registers, to which we now turn.

B. ROMAN CATHOLIC REGISTERS

As we have seen, Roman Catholicism was subject to penal legislation between the sixteenth and the nineteenth century, and especially in the earlier centuries. The compilation of registers of baptisms, marriages and burials was therefore unwise. Discovery by the authorities could result in prosecution for those named in them. Even when that threat had eased, many priests did not bother to keep records. The keeping of registers was not seen as a priority.

There are no known registers from the reigns of Elizabeth and the first two Stuarts. The lack of them posed a serious problem for Catholics, not just in terms of inheritance, but also in terms of the practice of their own faith. Written proof of baptism was required for a variety of ecclesiastical purposes, for example ordination. In the absence of such proof, Catholics seeking ordination first had to undergo a conditional baptism.[23] The earliest registers consequently record baptisms only. Marriage and burial entries may commence decades later.

In addition to vital events, Roman Catholic registers frequently included other extraneous matter, such as lists of confirmees, converts and communicants. These will be discussed in Chapter 10.

The earliest register known is that of St Peter's Franciscan Mission, Birmingham, which has been published.[24] Another early register was compiled in the privileged security of the Chapel Royal, and began in 1662.[25] A handful of registers are known from the later seventeenth century,[26] but they only become common from the mid-eighteenth century. Many do not commence until the nineteenth century. About forty Catholic registers have survived from before 1770.[27] They were frequently kept in a higgledy-piggledy manner. The register of Revd Monox Hervey, for example, is written on sheets of paper which would be impossible to bind to make a uniform book.[28]

Early registers were the personal possessions of priests, rather than of the congregations whose members were recorded in them. Priests frequently took their registers with them when they moved to a new district; consequently, some registers include entries for people living in widely separated areas. Hervey's register, for example, which runs from 1729 to 1756, included entries from Heythrop (Oxfordshire), London, Ugthorpe (Yorkshire), York Castle and Welshpool (Montgomeryshire). Even if they were confined to one locality, that locality was likely to be wide in extent. For example, the register of Little Malvern Court (Worcestershire) mentions thirteen Anglican parishes, ranging from Ledbury (Herefordshire) to Newent (Gloucestershire).[29]

Most Catholic registers were written in Latin; indeed, this practice intensified after Catholic emancipation in 1829, and especially after the subsequent introduction of printed forms for the purpose. This should not, however, be a problem; Latin words such as *baptizatus erat*, *nupti erat* and *sepultus erat* are easily interpreted, and constantly repeated.

There was no standard format for entries in Roman Catholic registers, at least until the introduction of printed forms. Baptismal entries sometimes give dates of birth as well as of baptism (although frequently they were identical). They are likely to record the place of birth, and the mother's maiden name. They almost always name godparents (sometimes referred to as 'sponsors'). Sometimes, much more information is given. Since the late nineteenth century, it has been common to annotate baptismal entries with the dates of subsequent marriages. The number and frequency of baptisms recorded in a mission register is a good guide to the size of the mission's congregation.

SOME TYPICAL ENTRIES FROM ROMAN CATHOLIC REGISTERS

'Mark Kemply, lawfull Son of Thos Kemply labourer of Holme and his wife Ann, was born on the 14th day of Sept. 1781, and baptizd in ye absence of a pastor of that Congreg on ye 15th of ye same Month. He had for Sponsors John Howe and Mrs Haley'. [Holme on Spalding Moor]

'On ye 29th of January 1741/2 William Surr of the Parish and Town of Holme, Farmer, and Tenant to Mr Langdale, took for his lawfull Wife Jane Rose of the N. Riding from somewhere about Kilvington but at present of Holme, and received ye nuptial Benediction in presence of Thomas Garstang, Mary Robinson, Mary Barnes, and several other Witnesses'. [Holme on Spalding Moor]

'Peter Challoner young Lad died with Consomption of the 28 march, buried on 31, 1812, at Welsh Brick. Blessed with all the writes of the Church'. [Courtfield, Monmouthshire]

'[1821] February the 6 Died at Chelmsford Mary Elizabeth Dauther of Henry finch and Mary, his wife [alias wood] was Buried. By me under Signed. the child aged of 6 years, A. Danneville. the Body carred to Margueretting'. [Crondon Park, Essex]

Marriage entries similarly follow no set format, although they can provide much useful information, as the entry for William Surr in the box above demonstrates. In the register of Cheam, even the date and place of the Anglican ceremony is noted.[30] Nineteenth-century printed registers may provide such information as the parties' places of birth, the name of a widow's first husband, details of dispensations for consanguinity, and the names of all four grandparents.

Hardwicke's Marriage Act of 1753 had a major impact on Catholic registers. As noted above, it meant that Catholics were obliged to have their marriages celebrated twice if they wished to satisfy both the law of the land and their own church. Many Catholic marriages were registered in both Anglican and Roman Catholic registers. That was not, however, always the case. Some Catholic priests decided that it was no longer necessary to keep a register. Their decision may have been influenced by the fact that, as pointed out above, if the Roman ceremony took place first, they could be punished for acting illegally.

Bishop Challoner noted that the 'inferior sort' frequently did not bother with Anglican ceremonies.[31] At Tisbury (Wiltshire) there were numerous baptisms of children registered in the Wardour Roman Catholic register whose parents' marriages were not recorded in the Anglican registers.[32] The Catholic Lord Arundel was resident, and could protect his tenants.

Many Catholic marriage registers commence in the 1770s and 1780s. Those commencing in the early nineteenth century are not uncommon. It was not until the Civil Registration Act 1836 that the unsatisfactory position in which Hardwicke's Act had placed the Catholics was resolved. The Act relieved them of the threat of penalty, and enabled them to register their chapels for the conduct of marriages, although it was for the time being necessary for a registrar to be present.

Despite the fact that marriages were recorded in the civil registers, Catholic registers continued to be kept by some priests. Indeed, it is possible that a few Roman Catholic marriages went unrecorded in the civil registers even after 1836. However, it should be noted that many chapels, especially those which had no parochial function, did not register with the Registrar General. Marriages were not conducted in them.

After 1898, the attendance of the registrar at a Catholic marriage ceased to be required. Roman Catholic priests began to keep duplicate registers on printed forms, in the same way that Anglican clergymen did. One copy was for the church, one for the Registrar (when the forms in it had been filled in), and a transcript was regularly sent to the Registrar General.[33]

Mixed-faith marriages were a constant problem for both Roman Catholics and Protestants. Marriage outside of the faith was regarded as sinful by Catholics unless a dispensation was obtained, and was thought by Anglicans to lead to the 'perverting' of the partner and any children to Catholicism. Nevertheless, dispensations were obtained, and such marriages are sometimes recorded in Catholic registers, or in separate convalidation registers.[34] When John Winder and Anne Byron married at St Peter's, Lancaster, in 1805, the priest noted that he had conducted the ceremony 'against my principles relative to the marriage of Protestants & Catholics'. However, he justified himself by noting in the register 'NB Anne Winder afterwards became a Catholic'.[35]

The great majority of Catholic burials, as already noted, took place in Church of England churchyards. After 1852, many also took place in municipal burial grounds. Therefore, few burials are recorded in Catholic registers. Even if a priest commenced registering burials, his successors might not keep it up.

Where burial registers were kept, printed forms were in use from the mid-nineteenth century. These required both death and burial dates to be entered. They also state where burial took place. Funeral services were frequently conducted at home, so registers may record '*a domo*'.

Where a chapel had its own burial ground, it was more likely to keep a register. One of the earliest known Catholic burial grounds was opened at Harkirke (Lancashire) after a Catholic had been refused burial in 1611. The first entry in its register reads:

first of all, Wm Mathewson, an ould man of ye Morehowses wthin little Crosbie, dyed a Catholicke, the sixt daye of Aprill anno Doi 1611, and was buried in ye Harkircke ye day following, being Sonday, and ye 7 day of Aprill aforesaid, being first dened burial at Sephton Churche by the parson thereof.[36]

Such burial grounds were illegal. After the Sefton parson's veto on burials was withdrawn, the landowner was threatened with a fine of £2,000, and the burial ground was desecrated. He eventually had his fine reduced to £250, still a considerable sum of money. The burial ground continued in use, despite the desecration.[37] But few members of the laity used it; most of those buried after the fine was imposed were priests.

It was not until the 1852 Burial Act that Catholic burial grounds became legal, although it had become common in the early nineteenth century for a Catholic chapel to have a graveyard attached. It was not until the Burial Laws Amendment Act 1880 that the use of burial rites other than those of the established church were permitted in Church of England churchyards. Catholic burial grounds existing in 1831 may be recorded in the clergymen's returns to the 1831 census, now in the National Archives, class HO 71.

Locating Catholic Registers

Catholic registers of the nineteenth century and earlier have been deposited in many of the record offices mentioned in Chapter 3. They also hold numerous transcripts and microfilms of registers held elsewhere. Details of their holdings can frequently be found by consulting the Discovery union catalogue **http://discovery.national archives.gov.uk**. Full listings of Roman Catholic registers are included in the county volumes of the Society of Genealogists' *National Index of Parish Registers*. For a detailed national listing, see:

• Gandy, M. *Catholic Missions and Registers*. 6 vols + atlas vol. Michael Gandy, 1993.

Find My Past has recently digitised the sacramental registers held by the archives offices of Westminster[38] and Birmingham Archdioceses; the former include some embassy registers (see below), and many private registers kept by priests. See:

• England Roman Catholic Parish Congregational Records **http://search.findmypast.co.uk/search-world-Records/england-roman-catholic-parish-congregational-records**

Some record office websites provide separate lists of registers held . Northumberland Archives, for example, list numerous transcripts and microfilm, as well as original registers:

• Northumberland Archives: Roman Catholic Registers **www.experiencewoodhorn.com/file/uploaded/Collections% 20User%20Guides/ROMAN%20CATHOLIC%20REGISTERS.pdf**

Transcripts and facsimiles of registers held by the City of Westminster Archives Centre are listed by:

• Westminster City Archives Information Sheet 2: Roman Catholic Registers **http://transact.westminster.gov.uk/docstores/publications_ store/archives/info_sheets/info_sheet_2_catholic_registers.pdf**

A few registers are in the National Archives, and have been digitised for the internet. When the Registrar General invited non-Anglican churches to deposit their registers in 1841, and again in 1857, most Roman Catholics refused. Priests needed ready access to them in order to be able to provide certificates of baptism, confirmation and marriage. Candidates for ordination needed certificates of baptism and confirmation; so did couples wishing to marry.[39] Catholic marriages conducted between 1753 and 1837 were legally invalid; priests were understandably unwilling to supply the authorities with evidence of their illegalities.

Despite these objections, a few Catholic registers were deposited, and are now in the National Archives, class RG 4. Most are from northern England, as the Vicar Apostolic of the Northern District insisted that registers should be deposited. Of the seventy-eight Roman Catholic registers deposited, seventy came from his district.[40] Some of the priests concerned made copies of the surrendered registers for their own use. The deposited registers are now available, fully indexed, on a pay-per-view database:

• BMD Registers
  www.bmdregisters.co.uk

The Family History Library of the Latter Day Saints holds microfilm of many Roman Catholic registers, which are indexed by:

• International Genealogical Index
  www.familysearch.org/search/collection/igi.

Indexes and transcripts of Roman Catholic registers can be found on many websites. See, for example:

• Liverpool History Projects
  www.liverpoolhistoryprojects.co.uk
  Includes databases of baptisms, marriages and burials
• MLFHS Catholic Register Index
  www.mlfhs.org.uk/data/catholic_search.php
  For Manchester

Many registers have been published by the Catholic Record Society **http://catholicrecordsociety.co.uk/publications/records-series** and the Catholic Family History Society **http://catholicfhs.online/ index.php/publications.html**. A few are included in *Phillimore's Parish Register* series of publications. Others have been published by Shropshire Parish Register Society, Staffordshire Parish Register Society, and, more recently, a number of family history societies. Many transcripts made by the Catholic Family History Society are held by the Catholic National Library (see above, p.56), and are listed by:

- Catholic National Library Mission Registers
  http://catholicfhs.online/images/cfhs/CNatinalLibrary/ Catholic-NationalLibraryMissionRegisters.pdf

Steel's work[41] lists published registers (although many have been published since it was compiled). For an index to Catholic marriage registers, mainly covering London and Essex, and also including a few baptisms (mainly adult), see:

- *The Anstruther Catholic marriage and baptism index*. CD/Fiche. Parish Register Transcription Society/Institute of Heraldic and Genealogical Studies, 2005.

See also:

- Adolph, A.R.J.S. 'The Catholic Marriage Index', *Family History*, 16(129), NS. 105, 1991, p. 10-14.

Although Catholic registers are supposed to be deposited in Catholic diocesan archives seventy years after the last entry in them, they are usually closed to public consultation for 110 years from the date of their compilation. They are private sacramental records. Priests are expected to add supplementary, and potentially sensitive, information to the entries in them. Some of these additions are discussed in chapter 10.

C. EMBASSY REGISTERS

Registers were kept by chaplains of foreign embassies. They frequently allowed English Catholics to join in worship, although technically that was illegal, and there were occasions in the sixteenth and seventeenth century when worshippers were arrested as they left embassies. One Sunday morning in 1606, the Spanish ambassador's house was 'beset with constables sergeants and such like worshipful officers to apprehend all such as come out from thence when mass was ended'. Twenty-six were taken and imprisoned; however, seventy remained inside until the ambassador's protest at the 'dishonour offered him to beset his house in such disgraceful manner' caused the siege to be lifted.[42]

Attendance remained illegal in the eighteenth century, but enforcement became laxer. The registers of these chapels record many baptisms and marriages of English subjects of the crown. A number are held by Westminster Diocesan Archives, as noted above. Some have been published; see, for example:

• Lindsay, Claude Reginald. 'The Catholic Registers of the Church at Lincoln's Inn Fields, London: an instalment of baptisms and marriages from 1759, with collections of previous entries'. *Miscellanea 11*. Catholic Record Society 19. 1917, p.202-404. The Sardinian Embassy Chapel.

Lincolns Inn Roman Catholic Chapel.

• Weale, J. Cyril M., ed. *Registers of the Catholic Chapels Royal and of the Portuguese Embassy Chapel, 1662-1829.* Catholic Record Society 38. 1941. Marriages only.

D. MONUMENTAL INSCRIPTIONS

A substantial number of tombstones memorialising Catholics can be found in Anglican churches and churchyards. Those of the gentry and aristocracy were frequently placed in prominent positions. These memorials originally had to conform to Protestant sensitivities, and avoided mention of topics such as prayers for the dead or depictions of the cross. Explicit expressions of Catholic faith in the penal years are rare, although a handful can be found; for example, John Yate, of Buckland (Berkshire), who died in 1658, was declared on his tombstone to have been '*in Sanctae Romanae Ecclesiae Communione*'.[43] More frequently, eighteenth-century Catholic tombstones can be recognised by the absence of pagan cherubs, urns, torches, and similar imagery, which were characteristic of the century, and by the presence of the monogram IHS, the middle letter perhaps surmounted by a cross so insignificant in size that it escaped notice. These are frequently accompanied by the three nails and surrounded by rays. Sometimes these are engraved within the shape of a heart, alluding to the sacred heart of our Lord. In the nineteenth century, as a consequence of the Oxford Movement, the cross and the monogram also began to be used by Protestants, but by then Roman Catholics were able to include previously forbidden items. Crosses became larger, and increasingly stood alone on Catholic monuments. But the real give away is the presence of prayers for the dead, which would not be found on non-Catholic inscriptions (at least until the late nineteenth-century), or the initials RIP (*Requiescat in Pace*).

Many monumental inscriptions from Gloucestershire, Hampshire, Herefordshire, Kent, Lincolnshire, Middlesex, Monmouthshire and Yorkshire, are recorded in:

• Matthews. John Hobson. 'Catholic memorial inscriptions', in *Obituaries.* Catholic Record Society, 12. 1913, p.232-72.

Names from monumental inscriptions at the Bar Convent, York, are listed by:

- Belt, A. 'Monumental Inscriptions in the Cemetery of the Bar Convent, York', *Catholic Ancestor* 5(5), 1995, p.207-9.

A few collections of Catholic inscriptions have been published by family history societies. For example, the *Baddesley Clinton St Francis Of Assisi Roman Catholic Church Monumental Inscriptions* are available on fiche from the Birmingham & Midland Society for Genealogy and Heraldry. It is worth checking the publications pages of family history society websites to see what is available. Society websites are listed at **www.ffhs.org.uk/members2/contacting.php**.

E. THE COLLEGE OF ARMS REGISTER

The problems caused by the inability of the Church of England to register the baptisms, marriages and burials of every subject of the Crown led to a number of remedial attempts to create alternative registries. The most successful of these were the Wesleyan Metropolitan Registry, and the Protestant Dissenters Registry.[44] For obvious reasons, neither of these were used by Roman Catholics. However, the registry of births established at the College of Arms in 1747 was used by some prominent Catholic families.

The Registry was not a great success. Only three volumes were actually used, and only 224 births were recorded. One volume recorded events that took place before 1747, although none of Roman Catholics. Another volume included births from 1747 to 1793, and records 160 births, including many Catholics. A third volume was intended to record colonial entries, but there are only three entries in it. The form of entry used in the second volume included much more detail than is found in other registers. Entries included the names of grandparents and even one great-grandparent. Steel provides a detailed discussion of this register, which is still held by the College of Arms.[45]

Chapter 6

ROMAN CATHOLIC CHARITIES AND SOCIETIES

A. GENERAL

Many charities have supported the work of the Roman Catholic Church, especially in areas such as education, social work, youth work, emigration and spiritual provision. In the nineteenth century, the church was primarily a church for the poor. That is reflected in the diversity of Catholic charities. The larger ones have sometimes been concerned with a wide range of issues; for example, the Westminster Diocesan Education Fund has supported orphanages and emigration as well as schools. The provision of schooling will be discussed in Chapter 7.

The archives of Catholic charities include much information relevant to family and local history researchers. They have been little used. For general discussions of Catholic charities, see:

- Pinches, Sylvia. 'Church charities in the Diocese of Birmingham, 1800-1918', *Catholic Ancestor* 8(1), 2000, p.28-36.
- Pinches, Sylvia M. 'Lay charities in the Diocese of Birmingham, 1800-1918', *Catholic Ancestor* 8(2), 2000, p.73-83.

A list of 150 lay societies is provided by:

- Gard, Robin. 'Catholic Lay Societies in England and Wales 1870-1970: a preliminary list', *Catholic Archives* 10, 1990, p.48-57.

Archives of a small number of these societies are held by Westminster Diocesan Archives. See:

- Gard, Robin. 'The Survey of Records of Lay Societies: records in the Westminster Diocesan Archives', *Catholic Archives* 16, 1996, p.64-5.

For family historians, charities which ran orphanages and/or arranged the emigration of children, are of particular interest, and are discussed in general below. The archives of devotional societies frequently include lists of members. Charities concerned with the support of the clergy also left potentially useful archives.

It is not possible here to do more than flag up the fact that archives of charities do exist, and that they may be useful to both family and local historians. The notes on particular charities which follow are far from comprehensive; they are merely intended to give a flavour of what may be available among the archives of a wide range of other charities. Works describing the history and archives of a number of Catholic charities are listed by Gandy (1).

B. CATHOLIC ORPHANAGES

Catholics were particularly anxious to ensure that Catholic orphans were cared for by Catholics, and established a substantial number of children's homes. The first Catholic orphanage was opened at North Hyde (Middlesex) in 1847.[1] More rapidly followed. The Westminster Diocesan Education Fund (see below, p.150) supported a home for blind, deaf and dumb children at Boston Spa (Yorkshire) run by the Sisters of Charity of St Vincent de Paul.[2] Orphanage archives are likely to include registers, case files, minutes and annual reports, among other things. They are scattered, and can be found in many of the record repositories mentioned in Chapter 3. It is necessary to identify the relevant orphanage before you can search for a specific individual.

A general introduction to Catholic orphanages is provided by two of the essays in:

- Button, Marilyn, & Sheetz-Nguyen, Jessica A., eds. *Victorians and the Case for Charity: Essays on responses to English Poverty by the State, the Church, and the Literati.* McFarland & Co., 2014. This includes Sheetz-Nguyen, Jessica A. 'Father of the Orphan, his Helper and his Judge: Roman Catholic response to the English Poor Law System', and Egan, Moira E. 'Something for the Poor: London Women Religious and Social Reform in the 1840s'.

The Daughters of Charity of the St Vincent de Paul Society ran numerous children's homes in the late nineteenth and twentieth century. Records of the children in their care can be found in their surviving archives, which are listed by:

• Greville, Judith. 'Records of the Children's Homes of the Daughters Of Charity Of St Vincent De Paul', *Catholic Archives* 15, 1995, p.3-12. Updated by Greville, Judith. 'The Daughters of Charity and Children's Records', *Catholic Archives* 25, 2005, p.42-56.

A number of works include details of the records of specific institutions. For example, the annual reports of a Manchester orphanage, which include lists of orphans, are described by:

• Gandy, Michael. 'St Bridget's Catholic Female Orphan Asylum for Manchester and Salford (founded 1840)', *Catholic Ancestor* 6(2), 1996, p.81-4.

A number of Roman Catholic institutions are among the homes listed by:

• Former Children's Homes
  www.formerchildrenshomes.org.uk

  See also:

• Limbrick, Gudrun Jane. *How to Research Childhoods spent in former children's homes, orphanages, cottage homes and other children's institutions.* WordWorks, 2013.

C. EMIGRATION

In the nineteenth and early twentieth century, many philanthropists thought that emigration to the colonies promised the best future for orphans and other poor children. Father Nugent and his Nugent Society Care Homes were the first to send children to Canada. Archives relating to British Home Children and other institutions formerly run by Nugent Care have been deposited at Liverpool Record Office **http://liverpool. gov.uk/archives**, although some more recent admittance registers are retained by the charity. For details, see:

- Nugent Care: Access to Records
  www.wearenugent.org/contact/access-to-records

For the work of the Catholic Emigration Society, which sent many children to Canada in the late nineteenth century, see:

- McClelland, V. Alan. 'The Making of Young Imperialists: Rev. Thomas Seddon, Lord Archibald Douglas, and the re-settling of British Catholic Orphans in Canada', *Recusant History* 19(4), 1989, p.509-29.

See also:

- Gandy, Michael. 'The Catholic Emigration Society', *Catholic Ancestor* 3(3), 1990, p.116-7.

After the Custody of Children Act 1891, which legalised the work of private emigration societies, Catholic child migration became focused through the Archdiocese of Westminster's 'Crusade of Rescue' in 1899. Between the 1870s and the 1920s the Westminster Diocesan Education Fund sent over 50,000 children to Canada (although not all of them were Catholic). They have been listed by the Catholic Family History Society.

The Catholic Children's Society **www.cathchild.org.uk/our-services/post-adoption** holds the records of a number of its predecessor societies. These include records relating to homes and migration schemes in both Canada and Australia, including a database of children who went overseas 1938–63, and a collection of registers of Catholic workhouse children 1870–1920, as well as other administrative records.[3]

For other material relating to child migration to Canada, visit:

- British Home Children in Canada
  http://canadianbritishhomechildren.weebly.com

See also:

- Library and Archives Canada: Catholic Organizations
  www.bac-lac.gc.ca/eng/discover/immigration/immigration-records/home-children-1869-1930/home-children-guide/Pages/catholic-organizations.aspx

D. GUILDS, FRATERNITIES AND SODALITIES

There were numerous Catholic guilds, fraternities and sodalities; many social and devotional activities were based on them.[4] Some of these organizations operated throughout the country, for example, the Society of St Vincent de Paul (for laymen), the Daughters of Charity (for lay women) and the Sodality of the Children of Mary (for girls). Others were more local in character. By 1880, almost every Catholic parish had at least one of these organisations attached to it. Their records (frequently kept with other parish records) contain a great deal of information for family and local historians. Among the records of Preston English Martyrs Church, for example, is a St Vincent de Paul relief book, giving details of the poor visited by its members, 1889–96. There is also an 'admission certificate book' for the Third Order of St Francis, dating from around 1889–1978.[5] Devotional societies frequently recorded the deaths of their members, so that they could be prayed for.

E. CLERGY AND MISSION FUNDS

Many funds were established to support local clergy and missions. For example, the Hampshire Secular Clergy Fund aimed to increase the salary of the Winchester incumbent, to pay for masses for the soul of the founder, to relieve the poor, to apprentice poor children and to pay for poor burials in St James's Cemetery, Winchester. For its accounts, see:

- 'The Hampshire Secular Clergy Fund rules and the Hampshire ledger', in Scantlebury, Robert, ed. *Hampshire registers (and Dorset), II.* Catholic Record Society, 43. 1949, p.1-86. Covers 1682-1793.

A fund for the secular clergy in the north is described by:

- Gooch, Leo. 'The Northern Brethren Fund', *Northern Catholic History* 21, 1985, p.6-12.

For the rules of another northern fund, see:

- Alger, Brendan. 'The Lancashire and Westmorland Clergy Fund I', *North West Catholic History* 3, 1971, p.75-86.

F. INDIVIDUAL SOCIETIES[6]
Aged Poor Society
This society, established in 1708, supported poor Catholics of good character. It provided pensions, and, in 1851, established St Joseph's Almshouses in Hammersmith. Minute books and annual reports are held by London Metropolitan Archives **https://search.lma.gov.uk** from 1820. No earlier records are known. For details, visit:

• Aged Poor Society
  www.ucl.ac.uk/bloomsbury-project/institutions/aged_poor.htm

The names and addresses of pensioners in 1851 and 1861 are extracted from its annual reports by:

• Moretti, Colin. 'The Aged Poor Society and Saint Joseph's Almshouse', *Catholic Ancestor* 10(3), 2004, p.89-97.

Casey's Charity
Over 13,000 poor Catholics of Manchester benefited from the charity established by John Casey in 1794. See:

• Butler, Tom. 'Casey's Charity for the Poor Catholicks of Manchester', *Catholic Ancestor* 6(5), 1997, p.202-9.

The charity's account book, listing the names of beneficiaries, is available on CD:

• *The Account Book of Casey's Charity: an indexed transcript 1794-1847*. CD. Manchester and Lancashire Family History Society, [199-]?

Catholic Missionary Society
The Catholic Missionary Society was founded in 1910 in order to reach out to non-Catholics, especially high church Anglicans, and to the lapsed. It ceased to operate in 2003. Its archives, which include papers relating to missionary priests, are held in Westminster Diocesan Archives **http://rcdow.org.uk/diocese/archives**.

Nugent Care

This charity's emigration activities have already been discussed. It also ran a number of children's homes in Liverpool and the North West. In addition to the charity's own administration, its archives at Liverpool Hope University include the papers of Father Nugent relating to his time as chaplain of Walton Gaol, and as co-founder of the Liverpool Catholic Children's Protection Society, together with the letters of Monsignor John Bennett, which deal with topics such as child welfare, juvenile delinquency, child psychology, and the end of child emigration to Canada. For a description and a presentation on the archive, see respectively:

• Nugent Care Archive, 1864-2006
  http://archiveshub.ac.uk (search 'Nugent Care')
• Nugent Care Archives; Liverpool Hope University
  http://slideplayer.com/slide/9781556/

St Joseph's Missionary Society

In 1866, St Joseph's College of the Sacred Heart for Foreign Missions was opened at Mill Hill; the Mill Hill fathers subsequently founded this society. For its history, and for contact details, visit:

• Mill Hill Missionaries: St Joseph's Missionary Society
  www.millhillmissionaries.co.uk

The Society's archives include much information about individual missionaries, and about their work. They are discussed by:

• Mol, William. 'The Archives of the Mill Hill Missionaries', *Catholic Archives* 2, 1982, p.20-27. See also 16, 1996, p.12-20.

Chapter 7

SCHOOLS, COLLEGES AND SEMINARIES

A. CATHOLIC SCHOOLS UNDER THE PENAL LAWS

From 1559 until 1869, schoolmasters required a bishop's licence in order to teach. Catholics were forbidden to teach, so could not obtain one.[1] Catholic schooling in England was therefore difficult to obtain. Those who could afford it paid a private Catholic tutor (frequently a priest), or sent their children to the Continent. Nevertheless, it has been possible to identify over 120 clandestine schoolmasters in the seventeenth century, and another 135 in the eighteenth century. For example, in 1635 William Hill of Fareham had twenty pupils, 'many of them gentlemens sons of good qualitie, and out of severall partes and quarters of the realm'.[2] His school was closed down by the authorities. During Elizabeth's reign, twenty-three schoolmasters were executed.[3] Many sources have been used to compile:

- Beales, A.C.F. 'A Biographical Catalogue of Catholic Schoolmasters in England, 1558-1700. Part 1:1558 – 1603', *Recusant History, 7*, 1963, p.268-89. No more published.

For additions and corrections, see:

- McCann, Timothy J. 'Catholic schoolmasters in Sussex 1558-1603: addenda and corrigenda to Beales's Catholic Schoolmasters', *Recusant History* 12(2), 1974, p.235-7.
- Tobias, J. 'Warwickshire addenda and corrigenda to Beales's Catholic schoolmasters' *Recusant History* 10(2), 1969, p.119-20.

In addition to the schoolmasters themselves, a number of institutions were founded in penal times and managed to survive. There were Catholic schools in England from the 1660s: Holywell (Lancashire), Osmotherley and Quosque (Yorkshire), Twyford and Silkstead (Hampshire), Wolverhampton (Staffordshire) and Hammersmith (Middlesex).[4] Bishop Challoner founded two schools for boys, at Standon Lordship (Hertfordshire) in 1749, and Sedgley Park (Staffordshire). For girls, the Bar Convent of the Institute of the Blessed Virgin Mary in York[5] ran a boarding school, and opened a day school for local girls in 1699. These establishments were fortunate to survive; many other schools were 'discovered' by the authorities and closed down. In 1635, for example, in addition to the school at Fareham mentioned above, schools at Stanley Grange (Derbyshire), and Willenhall (Staffordshire) suffered this fate.[6] On the other hand, imprisoned Catholic priests taught school in the Elizabethan gaols of York and Hull![7]

The eighteenth century witnessed the growth of private and charity schools in England serving the new Catholic middle classes. Many village schools run by the 'Papists' are mentioned in the Anglican replies to bishops' queries. There was also a tolerable system of catechising in the Catholic missions.[8]

For a detailed account of Catholic 'education under penalty', listing unpublished sources, see:

- Beales, A.C.F. *Education under Penalty: English Catholic Education from the Reformation to the fall of James II, 1547-1689.* Athlone Press, 1963.

Chapters on the leading schools of the nineteenth century and earlier are included in:

- Barnes, Arthur Stapylton. *The Catholic Schools of England.* Williams and Norgate, 1926.

B. THE CONTINENTAL SEMINARIES
It was virtually an unwritten law in early modern England that parents should determine the upbringing of their children. Although the government made various attempts to remove children from Catholic parents, and to supervise their education, none succeeded to any great extent.[9] Lord Burghley attempted to use the Court of Wards to ensure

that orphans from Catholic families were brought up as Protestants, but nevertheless the wardships of many such orphans were sold to their Catholic relatives.[10]

Roman Catholics who could afford it sent their children to the English colleges on the Continent. These institutions were founded to train priests. In practice, they catered for lay boys as well. Not everyone who attended a continental seminary was intending to be ordained. Only a quarter of Douai students were ordained in the 1750s and 1760s.[11] Boys destined for both lay and clerical vocations were educated together throughout the penal years, and indeed after the return to England in the 1790s. Girls were also catered for: the earliest continental girl's school was St Ursula's School at Louvain, opened as early as 1548.[12] By around 1600 there were well over 400 students on the Continent.[13]

The education provided by continental institutions was much better than that available to English Protestants. This superiority was probably one of the reasons why Catholics made a far greater contribution to English intellectual life than their numbers warranted.[14] Indeed, it was not unknown for Protestant children to be given a Catholic continental education. In 1766, a correspondent of the *Gentleman's Magazine* was horror-struck to discover some fifty Protestant English girls being educated in a Calais convent. By this date, perhaps as many as 750 English children were receiving a continental Catholic education.[15]

The principal seminaries were those at Douai and Rome; the largest school was that at St Omer. The Spanish and Portuguese institutions were all fairly small and insignificant, effectively annexes to their larger compatriots. Much information on the seminaries and schools in the Low Countries is provided by:

• Guilday, P. *The English Catholic Refugees on the Continent. Vol. 1: The English colleges and convents in the Catholic Low countries, 1558-1795.* Longmans Green & Co., 1914. No more published.

Much information concerning English students at continental seminaries can be found in the *responsa* that students sometimes compiled when entering them. These *responsa* could be, in effect, mini-biographies, indicating matters such as their parentage and their status. Those from the English College at Rome were collected for almost a century, and have been published (see below, p.141). Similar information was collected at Douai and Valladolid for shorter periods.

Information on the history and archives of some of the major institutions is provided below. Many other works on the history of the continental seminaries are listed by Gandy (1).

Bornhem

This was a Dominican school established in 1660 for the education of lay boys.[16] Its conventual register includes the names of many boys at the school, and also of those who came into contact with Dominican missionaries in England:

• Jarrett, Bede, ed. 'Rosary Confraternity lists', *Miscellanea 9.* Catholic Record Society 14. 1914, p.204-36.

Dieulouard

A Benedictine College was founded at Dieulouard in 1658. The school remained small until the monks fled to Acton Burnell in 1793, and subsequently established themselves at Ampleforth. For a list of students, see:

• Aveling, Hugh. 'Pensioners at the Benedictine College at Dieulouard (1619–1756)', *Recusant History* 5(1), 1959, p.35-9.

Douai College

The College at Douai, founded by William Allen in 1568, was the first continental seminary for English Catholics. The principal events in its history, including its removal to Rheims between 1578 and 1593, are recorded in the College 'diaries', most of which escaped destruction during the French Revolution.[17] These 'diaries' list the comings and goings of students and visitors, ordinations and deaths, as well as the events and routines of college life. The earliest includes an account of the founding of the College, the names of those ordained priests from 1573 to 1632, and the names of those sent to the English Mission from 1574 to 1644. Associated with it are various lists of students, dating from 1627 to 1780, who took the College oaths; these frequently include dates of birth, the names of parents and names assumed at College, as well as their respective dioceses. The second diary is accompanied by a variety of letters and other documents. Both these diaries, together with a variety of related documents, are printed in:

- Knox, Thomas Francis, ed. *The First and Second Diaries of the English College, Douay*. Records of the English Catholics under the Penal Laws, 1. David Nutt, 1878.

For later diaries, see:

- Burton, E.H.; Williams, T.L. eds. *The Douay College Diaries, Third, Fourth and Fifth, 1598-1654, with the Rheims Report, 1579-80.* 2 vols. Catholic Record Society Record Series 10-11. 1911.
- Burton, E.H., & Nolan, E. eds.*The Douay College Diaries: the Seventh Diary, 1715-78, preceded by a Summary of Events, 1691-1715.* Catholic Record Society Record Series 28 (1928)

Other diaries, lists of priests and alumni, and various other documents, are printed in:

- Harris, P.R., ed. *Douay college documents, 1693-1794.* Catholic Record Society Record Series, 63 (1972).

See also:

- Harris, P.R. 'The English College, Douai, 1750-1794', *Recusant History* 10, 1969, p.79-95.

Douai St Gregory's School

The seminary at Douai should not be confused with the Benedictine monks of St Gregory who settled there, quite separately, in 1605, establishing their school in 1608. It moved to Acton Burnell in 1794, and to Downside in 1814. Birt's history of the school mentions many names, gives brief biographical notes on 'Gregorian worthies', and lists school 'captains' 1856–1901 and headmasters, 1605–1902. See:

- Birt, Henry Norbert. *Downside: the History of St Gregory's School from its commencement at Douay to the present time*. Kegan Paul Trench Trübner & Co., 1902.

For St Gregory's boys, see:

• *List of boys at St Gregory's: Douay* . 1614-1793, Acton Burnell 1794-1814, Downside 1814-1972. Downside Abbey, 1972.

Ghent

The Benedictine nunnery at Ghent was founded from Brussels in 1624. The nuns ran a school for girls, which continued in England after they fled the Continent, closing in 1968. For its register, see:

• *The register of the Benedictine schools for girls at Ghent, Preston, Caverswall and Oulton, 1624-1969*. Occasional Publication 6. Catholic Family History Society, 2004.

Liège (See St Omer)

Lisbon

Lisbon College was founded in 1628, and closed in 1971. For its history, see:

• Johnson, Simon. *The English College at Lisbon, vol.1: From Reformation to Toleration*. Downside Abbey Press, 2014.

Lisbon College.

Its register is printed in:

• Sharratt, M. ed., *Lisbon College Register, 1628-1813*. Catholic Record Society Record Series, 72. 1991.

This also includes some information on the college's history and archives. For a discussion of the latter, which includes minutes, account books, visitation records, sermons and correspondence, as well as the register mentioned above, see:

• Sharratt, M. 'The Lisbon Collection at Ushaw', *Catholic Archives* 1, 1981, p.36-9. Reprinted from *Northern Catholic History* 8, 1978, p.30-36.

Madrid
The College at Madrid was founded in 1611, and closed when the Jesuits were expelled from Spain in 1767. Many letters, together with accounts, reports, and other documents, are printed in:

• Henson, Edwin, ed. *The English College at Madrid, 1611-1767*. Catholic Record Society, 29. 1929.

Paris
The purpose of St Gregory's College at Paris was to enable English Catholic priests and others to undertake higher theological study at the Sorbonne. These were picked men, and their numbers were small; there were never more than half a dozen students in residence. Details of their comings and goings are recorded in:

• Burton, Edwin Hubert, ed. 'The Register book of St Gregory's College at Paris, 1667-1786'. *Miscellanea 11*. Catholic Record Society, 19. 1917, p.93-160.

Rome
The Venerable English College at Rome **www.vecrome.org/history.html** was founded in 1579, and continues to operate today. For its history, see:

- Williams, M.E. *The Venerable English College, Rome: a history, 1579-1979.* 2nd ed. Gracewing, 2008. This includes a catalogue of the College archives.
- Gasquet, Cardinal. *A History of the Venerable English College, Rome: an account of its origins and work from the earliest times to the present day.* Longmans Green & Co., 1920.

Among the College's archives is the *Liber ruber* – the register of its students. This is very detailed, including information on places of birth, names of parents, education, progress through the College, reception of Minor and Major orders, and sometimes (especially in the case of bishops) details of life after leaving the College. It is published in:

- Kelly, Wilfrid, ed. *Liber ruber Venerabilis Collegii Anglorum de Urbe.* Catholic Record Society, 37 & 40. 1940-43. Pt.1. 1579-1630. Pt.2. 1631-1783.

Student applications for admission are printed in:

- Kenny, Anthony, ed. *The 'Responsa Scholarum' of the English College, Rome.* Catholic Record Society Record Series, 54 -55. 1962-3. Pt.1. 1598-1621. Pt 2. 1622-85.

For obits, see:

- Gasquet, Cardinal. *Obit book of the Venerable English College of St. Thomas de Urbe.* Rome: The Venerabile, 1929.

The College's archives are described in:

- Briggs, Charles, & Whelan, Brendan. 'The Archives of the Venerable English College in Rome', *Catholic Archives* 7, 1987, p.3-5.

St Omer and Bruges
The Jesuit school at St Omer was found by Fr Robert Persons in 1593, in order to cater for the many lay boys who sought basic schooling, and also to prepare students for seminary admission. By the end of the sixteenth century, it catered for 100 boys. In the seventeenth century,

perhaps one in four of the boys became priests.[18] The school moved to Bruges in 1762, staying there until the suppression of the Jesuits in 1773. It then moved to Liège and was run by seculars. In 1794, it fled the advancing French armies, and was re-founded at Stonyhurst (see below, p.146). For a biographical dictionary of St Omer boys, see:

• Holt, Geoffrey, ed. *St Omers and Bruges Colleges, 1593-1773: a biographical dictionary*. Catholic Record Society 69. 1979.

See also:

• Trappes-Lomas, Richard. 'Boys at Liege Academy 1773-91, with the names of their parents or guardians, and the pensions paid through the procurator in London', *Miscellanea 8*. Catholic Record Society 13. 1913, p.202-13.

For a detailed history of the school, see:

• Chadwick, Hubert. *From St Omer to Stonyhurst: a history of two centuries*. Burns & Oates, 1962.

Seville
The English Jesuit College at Seville was founded in 1592. It merged with Valladolid in around 1770. A list of alumni, together with notes on archives and various documents, is included in:

• Murphy, Michael, ed. *St Gregory's College, Seville, 1592-1767*. Catholic Record Society Record Series, 73. 1992.

The College's early history is recounted by the founder in:

• Persons, Robert. 'Annals of the English College, Seville', ed. J.H. Pollen, in *Miscellanea 9*. Catholic Record Society 14. 1914, p.1-24.

Persons includes a list of early alumni, which has been revised by:

• Henson, Canon Edwin & Loomie, Albert J. 'A Register of the Students at St. Gregory's College, Seville, 1591-1605', *Recusant History*, 9(3), 1967, p.163-70.

Valladolid

This college was founded in 1589, and some archives survive from that date. The register of students has been published:

- Henson, Edwin, ed. *Registers of the English College at Valladolid 1589-1862.* Catholic Record Society 30. 1930.

For other archives, see:

- Williams, Michael E. 'A Guide to The Archives of St Alban's College, Valladolid, with some Historical Notes', *Catholic Archives* 4, 1984, p.36-9.

The history of the College is dealt with by:

- Williams, Michael E. *St Alban's College Valladolid: Four Centuries of English Catholic Presence in Spain.* Palgrave Macmilllan, 1986. Includes description of the College archives.

C. CATHOLIC EDUCATION IN NINETEENTH AND TWENTIETH-CENTURY ENGLAND 1: PUBLIC SCHOOLS AND SEMINARIES

The French Revolution was hostile to Catholicism. The property of church institutions was confiscated; clergy and the religious were imprisoned or exiled. Many English religious orders, schools, and seminaries fled to England, where they re-established themselves. Technically, this was still illegal under the Catholic Relief Act 1791, but enforcement measures were never taken.[19] The refugee schools and seminaries are now represented by Ampleforth, Downside, Ushaw and Ware.

The returnees also included a number of women's teaching orders: Canonesses, Dominicans, Benedictines, Franciscans and Poor Clares. A number of other teaching orders were established in the first half of the nineteenth century; by 1850 there were twenty different orders of nuns running convent schools for girls. These attracted the daughters of tradesmen and the lesser gentry.[20]

In the larger Missions, small private schools were frequently established with the encouragement of the local priest; sometimes the proprietors were his relatives. Although private, they too were seen as part of the mission of the church. Mostly they took boys up to the age of eleven; girls might be older.[21]

Detailed histories and published lists of alumni are available for most of the institutions founded or re-founded following the expulsion from France; some of these are listed here. Other works on these and later foundations are listed by Gandy (1).

Ampleforth
Ampleforth was founded by the Dieulouard Benedictines in 1802 as a school for boys. It is still active; its website has many papers digitised from journals, a list of boys entering the school 1803–1895, obituaries, and other pages (but little on the Abbey's archives):

• Ampleforth Abbey: Monastery, Library and Archives
  www.monlib.org.uk

Ampleforth.

Downside (see above, p.138)

Oscott
Oscott College was founded in 1794 as St Mary's College in Handsworth; it moved to Oscott in 1838. Originally it operated as both a seminary for priests and a school, although the two functions were separated in 1873. The school closed in 1889. The seminary moved to Olton (Warwickshire), but returned to Oscott when the school closed. It served as the Central Seminary for England between 1897 and 1909. It is currently the seminary for the Archdiocese of Birmingham. See:

- Champ, Judith F., ed. *Oscott College, 1838-1988: a volume of commemorative essays*. 1988, p.185-224. This includes lists of resident staff, and of clerical students, 1888-1988.

Oscott's archives (which include much information on former students) are now held in the Archdiocese's archives. For details, see:

- Rowlands, Marie. 'Oscott College Archives', *Catholic Archives* 23, 2003, p.56-60.
- Williams, Mary Harcourt. 'The Archives of St Mary's College, Oscott', *Catholic Archives* 30, 2010, p.12-21.

The College retains its Recusant Library, which includes many early Catholic publications. Visit:

- Oscott College: Glancey Library
  www.oscott.net

Ratcliffe College
Ratcliffe College **http://ratcliffe-college.co.uk/why-choose-ratcliffe/ institute-of-charity** was founded by the Rosminian Fathers' Institute of Charity in 1845 as a seminary, but became a boys' school in 1847. For its history, see:

- Leetham, C.R. *The History of Ratcliffe College, 1847-1947*. Ratcliffian Association, 1950. Includes list of students; also some masters and brothers.

Stonyhurst.

Stonyhurst
The Jesuit College at Stonyhurst descends from the College at St Omer founded in 1593 (see above, p.41–2). For its history, see:

• Muir, T.E. *Stonyhurst College 1593-1993*. James & James, 1992.

In addition to the archives of Stonyhurst itself, the College also holds a collection of medieval manuscripts, and much material relating to St Omer. The archives are described by:

• Turner, F.J. The Stonyhurst Archives', *Catholic Archives* 9, 1989, p.20-25. Reprinted in part from *North West Catholic History* 12, 1985, p.30-33.
• 'The Manuscripts in the Library of Stonyhurst College, belonging to the Society of Jesus', in *Royal Commission on Historical Manuscripts Second Report*. 1874, p.143-6. See also third report, 1872, p.334-41, and 10th report, 1885, p.25.

Ushaw
One group of the Douai seminarians settled at Ushaw College in 1808. For its history, see:

• Milburn, David, *A history of Ushaw College: a study of the origin, foundation and development of an English Catholic seminary, with an epilogue 1908-1962*. Durham: The Ushaw Bookshop, 1964. Includes a useful guide to Ushaw archives.

Many biographical notes on individuals associated with Ushaw are included in:

• *Records and Recollections of St Cuthbert's College, Ushaw …* Preston: E. Buller & Son, 1889.

The archives of the College are now in Durham University Library Special Collections. See:

• Bush, Jonathan. 'The Ushaw College archive', *Catholic Archives* 34, 2014, p.1-16.

Ware
Another group from Douai settled at Ware in 1793. St Edmund's College at Ware continued as a seminary and boys school until 1869, when the seminarians moved to Hammersmith. Seminarians returned, however, in 1904, and remained until 1975, when they moved to Chelsea, although retaining the name Allen Hall, which they had used at Ware. For its history, see:

• Schofield, Nicholas. *The History of St Edmund's College*. The Edmundian Association: 2013. Includes lists of presidents and headmasters.

Some records of St. Edmund's are held in the Westminster Diocesan Archives.

D. CATHOLIC EDUCATION IN NINETEENTH AND TWENTIETH CENTURY ENGLAND 2: THE EDUCATION OF POOR CATHOLICS

Most of the schools discussed thus far were public schools intended for the middle and upper classes. However, the restoration of the hierarchy in 1850 coincided with an increasing Catholic concern with the education of the poor.[22] For Cardinal Wiseman, the new Archbishop, such concern was not a fringe activity, but central to the exercise of Christian responsibility. The primary focus of Catholic education switched to the provision of elementary and industrial schools, and to the needs of Catholic children in secular institutions such as

Cardinal Wiseman.

workhouses and prisons. For the next half century, Catholic secondary education tended to be restricted to schools run by the religious orders, many of which have already been mentioned.

In the 1840s, it was calculated that there were about 65,000 poor Catholic children without schooling.[23] The great majority of Irish

Catholics were poor, and many spent time in workhouses and similar institutions. Many of them – perhaps a majority – became lapsed Catholics. The hierarchy considered it vital for the future that Catholic children should be taught and cared for in Catholic institutions. New elementary schools were regarded as more important than new churches; indeed, church services were frequently held in school premises. By 1887, the church supported thirteen schools for workhouse children in Westminster, and was also heavily involved in supporting Reformatory schools for children who had fallen foul of the law.

Catholic schools faced great difficulties, due to the poverty of their communities. They had to cope with poor attendance, a lack of resources and a lack of adequately trained teachers, especially male. Those which depended on government grant were regularly inspected. The sheer poverty of schools reduced their ability to be efficient, and a poor report could lead to a reduced grant, or perhaps its total withdrawal. Consequently, inspection day caused even more angst than Ofsted. Girls' schools run by nuns tended to be rated much more highly than boys' schools run by laymen.[24] Inspectors' reports can be found among the records of schools in local record offices.

A training college for teachers was founded at Hammersmith in 1850. Trainees' names are listed in the annual reports of the Catholic Poor Schools Committee, which also include the names of subscribers. The Committee, founded in 1847, coordinated the Church's educational work, but did not concern itself with secondary education. Its work was continued by the Catholic Education Council from 1905, and the Catholic Education Service from 1991. Its archives are held by St Mary's University, Twickenham, and are described by AIM25 **www.aim25.com**. Its journal, *The Catholic School*, published between 1848 and 1858, includes many lists of subscribers to particular schools. There is also a microfiche collection of its annual reports, 1848–1900, which can be found in some research libraries. See:

• Catholic Poor Schools Committee. *Annual Reports.* 71 fiche. EP Microform, 1979.

The work of the Catholic Poor Schools Committee, and of the schools which they supported, is introduced in:

- Marmion, John P. 'The Beginnings of the Catholic Poor Schools in England', *Recusant history* 17(1), 1985, p.67-83.

For a list of the schools supported by the Committee, taken from its second report, see:

- 'Catholic Schools c.1845', *Catholic Ancestor* 9(6), 2003, p.227-48.

The Committee worked closely with diocesan organisations. In 1866, Archbishop Manning issued his 'Education Pastoral', and followed it up by launching the Westminster Diocesan Education Fund. It was emulated by similar funds in other dioceses. The Fund's task was defined as being to erect, inspect, and maintain schools for the education of poor Catholic children, and to protect the faith of poor Catholic children in the care of secular institutions. Within a year of its foundation it had raised £7,855, and commenced twenty day schools.[25]

The Fund's activities in emigration and orphanages have already been mentioned (above, p.128 and 130). Its records are held by Westminster Diocesan Archives. Its annual reports contain many lists of children who received support. A few are listed in:

- 'Deaf, Dumb and Blind Children in Westminster', *Catholic Ancestor* 6(3), 1996, p.122-3.

Nuns' teaching orders supported the work of the Catholic Poor Schools Committee in their work with girls. Many convents conducted fee-paying schools for middle-class girls, and used the income to support poor schools. By 1950, there were no fewer than eighty-four different congregations of nuns involved in teaching children.[26]

Nuns also concerned themselves with the training of teachers. The Sisters of Notre Dame opened Our Lady's Training College for elementary teachers at Mount Pleasant in 1856. A number of training colleges for female secondary teachers were opened at the beginning of the twentieth century. For the educational work of nuns, see:

- Battersby, W.J. 'Educational work of the Religious Orders of Women, 1850-1950', in Beck, George Andrew, ed. *The English Catholics 1850-1950.* Burns Oates, 1950, p.337-64.

Parishes were closely involved in the running of Catholic schools. School log books can frequently be found among their archives. These log books enable us to study the day-to-day reality of late nineteenth-century Catholic school life, and to examine how education affected the lives of individual children. A number of Roman Catholic school logbooks and registers have been digitised at:

- National School Registers 1870–1914
  http://www.findmypast.com/school-registers

The Diocese of Westminster Archives holds various records of nineteenth- and twentieth-century schools and other children's institutions. See:

- Diocese of Westminster Archives Guide 4. Records of Schools and Childrens' Institutions
  http://rcdowarchives.blogspot.co.uk/p/family-history.html

Catholic teachers' names may also be found in the reports of Catholic Diocesan Boards of Education. These can usually be found among Catholic diocesan archives.

The Catholic Poor Schools Committee worked closely with government. The indigence of the Catholic community compelled reliance on government grants after they became available in 1846. Schools applying for grants between 1846 and 1924 had to submit preliminary statements, now in the National Archives class ED 7. These statements record information concerning the tenure and establishment of the school, its income and expenditure, and its accommodation and staffing. Schools were regularly inspected; inspectors' reports are frequently held with the records of individual schools by local record offices. For a detailed guide to educational records, see:

- Stephens, W.B., & Unwin, R.W. *Materials for the Local and Regional Study of Schooling, 1700-1900.* Archives and the user 7. British Records Association, 1987.

For a detailed discussion of the education of Catholic poor, see:

- Tenbus, Eric G. *English Catholics and the Education of the Poor 1847-1902.* Pickering & Chatto, 2010.

Chapter 8

THE CATHOLIC CLERGY

It is relatively easy to identify most Catholic clergy, despite the early practice of using aliases. All priests from 1558 to 1914 should be found in the two biographical works listed below, p.157. Priests in post in 1558 should be mentioned in the Clergy of the Church of England Database. There are biographical dictionaries covering most regulars. Many continental seminary registers have been published (see Chapter 7). Histories of particular missions usually include clergy lists. Many clergy were among the martyrs, whose lives have mostly been recounted in print.[1] A list of works on them is provided by Gandy (1).

A. MARIAN CLERGY IN 1558 AND AFTER

The separation of the Church of England from the Church of Rome was formalised by the 1559 Act of Uniformity. The oath of supremacy was tendered to all fourteen bishops, and many senior clergy. All but one of the bishops refused to take it, and were deprived. They remembered the failure of their predecessors to uphold Papal authority in 1553, and were not going to make the same mistake again.

Steel suggests that the 1559 Act resulted in the deprivation or resignation of perhaps 500 clergy.[2] Many others simply disappeared: in the Diocese of Lincoln the episcopal registers record almost 200 institutions without (as was normal) recording the reason for the vacancy.

The names of Marian priests who were deprived, resigned or simply disappeared can now easily be identified in:

• Clergy of the Church of England Database
  http://theclergydatabase.org.uk/

Cuthbert Mayne, Martyr.

There was not, however, an entirely black and white division between the deprived Roman Catholic priests and the Protestants, and this database does not necessarily provide conclusive proof of either tendency. A deprivation in 1559 could be due to Romanist tendencies – but priests could be deprived for a multitude of other reasons. Similarly, the fact that a priest remained at his post does not prove his Protestantism. Christopher Trychay, the priest of Morebath (Devon), clearly hoped for a restoration of the old religion. But he remained at his post until his death, seeing it as his duty to support his similarly conservative parishioners.[3]

A similar view was undoubtedly taken by some of the priests ordained by Bishop Tunstall of Durham before he was deprived by Elizabeth. Their careers are traced by:

- Forster, Ann. 'Bishop Tunstall's priests', *Recusant History* 9(4), 1968, p.175-204.

The Roman Catholic Church was also supported, to some extent, by the monks of the monasteries dissolved by Henry VIII. They had been pensioned off, and lists of their pensions still survive among the Exchequer's archives, for example, in class E 135. Pensions were still being paid during Elizabeth's reign. For Derbyshire, pensioners in Edward VI's reign are listed in:

- Cox, J. Charles. 'The Religious Pension Roll of Derbyshire, temp Edward VI', *Journal of the Derbyshire Archaeological and Natural History Society* 28, 1906, p.10-43.

B. THE SEMINARY PRIESTS AND THEIR SOCIAL ORIGINS
During Elizabeth's reign, there were roughly 800 English seminary priests, although only 471 can be shown to have worked in England.[4] Many never returned. Some died while studying; others were judged unfit to proceed to orders. There were a variety of opportunities for those who completed their studies. Some served elsewhere on the Continent: Englishmen filled a number of continental bishoprics and canonries. Others entered contemplative orders, or taught in the schools and seminaries. A few served as chaplains in the Spanish army.

More than half of those who did return to England were caught by the Elizabethan authorities; 123 were executed, while others endured long periods of imprisonment.[5] Forty converted to Anglicanism; some even became Anglican priests. A few lived under censure from the Roman authorities. It has not been possible to trace eighty of the priests who set out for the English mission.[6]

It has been estimated that there were around 300 priests active in England in 1603.[7] By 1640, that number had expanded to around 750, including perhaps 500 seculars, and substantial numbers of Jesuits and Benedictines, plus a few others. In 1640, there was perhaps one missioner for every eighty members of the laity; by 1770 there was one for every 200.[8] By 1820, numbers had reduced to perhaps 400 clergy; although a much smaller percentage of them were in religious orders.[9] The new seminaries at Oscott, Ushaw and Ware were only producing a trickle of new priests in the early years of the nineteenth century.

The origin of the Catholic clergy changed over the centuries. In the first four decades of the College at Douai, it had sufficient funds to provide scholarships for many poor students. Others were able to pay. Half of its students were the sons of gentlemen, and half came from other sectors of the community. In the years before the Restoration, funds were more limited, so a greater proportion of students were gentlemen. Scholarships began to be available again at the end of the seventeenth century, encouraging those of lower social status to enter the College; by 1750 almost half of the students were not paying fees.[10]

The ability of priests to perform their functions depended to some extent on their social origins. Plebeians could cope better than gentlemen with the privations that might be encountered on the open road serving a scattered congregation. Indeed, some gentle clergy considered that such a life was unbefitting for a clergyman.

In practice, during the penal era many priests were forced to seek the safety of gentlemen's houses, where they were expected to minister to the family and a few tenants, and to comply with their patrons' wishes, which were not necessarily mission orientated. Priests of plebeian origins were likely to be overawed in such circumstances. Mission consequently suffered. Many priests followed their patrons to London; consequently, some areas were without any clergy presence.

George Leyburn, the head of the English College at Douai in 1668, saw the need to recruit the sons of peers and the upper gentry. They were the only people capable of attempting to exercise authority over the gentry who sheltered priests.[11] However, the trend of recruitment was against Leyburn. By around 1740, the great majority of priests were not gentlemen.

C. SEMINARIES

In the penal period, priests were trained in the continental seminaries. These institutions returned to England during the French Revolution, and were discussed in Chapter 7. However, not all priests who served in nineteenth-century England were trained by them. The alumni of St Patrick's College, Maynooth, also played an important role in the nineteenth-century English mission. The college was founded by an Act of the Irish Parliament in 1795, and was controversially supported in the nineteenth century by UK parliamentary grant. Its alumni are listed in:

- Hamell, Patrick J. *Maynooth: Students and Ordinations Index 1795-1895.* [St Patricks College, Maynooth], 1982. A further volume covers 1895-1984.

  See also:

- Corish, Patrick J. 'Maynooth College Archives', *Catholic Archives* 13, 1993, p.46-8.

D. BISHOPS, ARCHPRIESTS, ETC

Until the restoration of the hierarchy in 1850, there were no dioceses for bishops to preside over. The Vicars Apostolic were bishops, but were consecrated to sees in *partibus infidelium*, that is, to the ancient sees which had been lost to Christianity by Muslim expansionism. Richard Challoner, for example, served as Bishop of Debra, and signed his letters as 'Ric.Ep.Debor' or 'Ric.Debor'. The Vicars Apostolic were in charge of mission districts, rather than dioceses, and were consequently unable to exercise all their episcopal powers.

The succession of the Vicars Apostolic, and of the post-1850 bishops, is given briefly by Gandy (1). For a more detailed account, including biographies of bishops, archpriests, and other senior clergy, see:

- Brady, W. Maziere. *Annals of the Catholic hierarchy in England and Scotland, A.D. 1585-1876, with dissertation on Anglican orders, including an account of the Archpriests, Prefects of Missions, Vicars Apostolic and Bishops of the Catholic Church of England and Scotland from the Extinction of the Ancient Hierarchy in Queen Elizabeth's reign to the present day.* Rome: Tipografia della Pace, 1877. London: John Mozley Stark, 1883.

  See also:

- Brady, W. Maziere. *The Episcopal Succession in England, Scotland and Ireland A.D.1400 to 1875.* Rome: Tipografia della Pace, 1878.

Bishops' biographies can also be found in the *Oxford Dictionary of National Biography* **www.oxforddnb.com**, and in:

• Plumb, Brian. *Arundel to Zabi: a biographical dictionary of the Catholic Bishops of England and Wales (deceased) 1623-1987.* 2nd ed. North West Catholic History Society, 2006. Downloadable from **www.nwcatholichistory.org.uk/publications/other-publications**

E. CHAPLAINS
In the second half of the nineteenth century, Roman Catholic chaplains were appointed in the army (from 1858), in poor law workhouses (from 1859), and in prisons (from 1863).[12] They can be traced in the records of these institutions.

F. BIOGRAPHICAL DICTIONARIES
The Catholic priesthood has been thoroughly listed in two works:

• Bellenger, Dominic Aidan. *English and Welsh Priests 1558-1800: A Working List.* Downside Abbey, 1984. List with dates of birth, profession, ordination, and death, also county of origin.
• Fitzgerald-Lombard, Charles. *English and Welsh Priests, 1801-1914: a working list.* Downside Abbey, 1993.

A more detailed biographical dictionary of the seminary priests is provided by:

• Anstruther, G. *The Seminary Priests, 1558-1850.* 4 vols. 1968-77. For a detailed review of this book see McGrath, P., & Rowe, J. 'Anstruther analysed: the English seminary priests', *Recusant history* 18(1), 1986, p.1-13.

A collection of eighteenth-century obituaries is transcribed in:

• Stanfield, Raymond. 'Obituaries of Secular Priests 1722-1783', in *Obituaries.* Catholic Record Society 12. 1913, p.1-15

The succession of priests in each mission is listed in:

• Kelly, Bernard. *Historical notes on English Catholic Missions.* Kegan Paul Trench Trübner & Co., 1907. Reprinted Michael Gandy, 1995.

For a regional biographical dictionary, see:

• Plumb, Brian. *Found Worthy: a Biographical Dictionary of the Secular Clergy of the Archdiocese of Liverpool (Deceased), 1850-2000.* 2nd ed. North West Catholic History Society, 2005. Downloadable from **www.nwcatholichistory.org.uk/members/other-publications**

Another regional biographical dictionary, with tables showing the succession of priests in particular missions, is included in:

• Oliver, George. *Collections illustrating the history of the Catholic Religion in the counties of Cornwall, Devon, Dorset, Somerset, Wilts, and Gloucester.* Charles Dolman, 1857.

Numerous biographies of sixteenth- and seventeenth-century martyrs (including some laymen) are included in:

• Challoner, Bishop. *Memoirs of missionary priests and other Catholics of both sexes that have suffered death in England on religious accounts, from the year 1577 to 1684*, ed. John Hungerford Pollen. New ed. Burns, Oates & Washbourne, 1924.

For refugees from the French revolution, see

• Bellenger, Aidan. *The French exiled clergy in the British Isles after 1789: an historical introduction and working list.* Downside Abbey, 1996.

A variety of other works on priests are listed by Gandy (1).

Chapter 9

RELIGIOUS ORDERS

Perhaps 5,000 Englishmen entered religious orders between 1598 and 1642.[1] Many more have been 'clothed' since then. In the nineteenth century, the revival of monasticism was an important feature in the Catholic advance. By 1950, there were more than seventy orders, with 2,360 priests.[2]

Monasticism was – and is – one of the great traditions of the church. Originally, monks followed the rule of St Benedict. Many other orders have since sprung up. In England, the Society of Jesus – the Jesuits – took the lead in the post-Reformation mission. In the nineteenth century, many regulars were deployed by the bishops in educational work. Their activities were discussed in Chapter 7.

For brief histories of the various orders, see:

• Steele, Francesca M. *Monasteries and Religious Houses of Great Britain and Ireland*. R. & T. Washbourne, 1903.

For a modern social history of nineteenth- and twentieth-century nuns, see:

• Walsh, Barbara. *Roman Catholic Nuns in England and Wales 1800-1937: A Social History*. Irish Academic Press, 2002.

An overview of nunneries in the nineteenth century, with chapters on each of the major orders, is provided by:

• Murphy, John Nicholas. *Terra incognita, or, the Convents of the United Kingdom*. Longmans, Green & Co., 1873.

For a database of nuns in various orders, together with copies of various related Catholic Record Society publications, and an 'archive calendar' listing many documents in continental repositories, see:

- Who Were the Nuns? A Prosopographical Study of the English Convents in Exile 1600-1800
  https://wwtn.history.qmul.ac.uk

Some 14,000 nuns, mainly of the nineteenth and twentieth centuries, are identified in:

- *Index of nuns.* CD. Catholic Family History Society, 2015.

A useful bibliography is included in:

- The History of Women Religious of Britain and Ireland
  https://historyofwomenreligious.org/

SPECIFIC ORDERS
Most works on monks and nuns deal with specific orders. The following notes deal with the major orders in which the English were active prior to around 1850. Twentieth-century orders have not been dealt with. Particular attention is given to archives. These notes are far from comprehensive. Many other works are listed by Gandy (1), who also provides a full list of the religious orders (for both men and women) which have been active in England.

Augustinians
Records of Augustinian canonesses are printed in:

- Hamilton, Adam. *The Chronicle of the English Augustinian Canonesses Regular of the Lateran, at St Monica's in Louvain (now at St Augustine's Priory, Newton Abbot, Devon), 1548 to 1625.* Sands & Co., 1904. Includes much genealogical information.
- Trappes-Lomax, Richard, ed. 'Records of the English Canonesses of the Holy Sepulchre of Liège, now at New Hall, 1652-1793', *Miscellanea 10.* Catholic Record Society, 17. 1915, p.1-247.

Benedictines

The English Benedictine Congregation, as has been seen, was reduced to a single member by 1600. However, Spanish and Italian monasteries had attracted many Englishmen, and by the early seventeenth century there were enough to establish several new English foundations. In 1607, St Gregory's was founded alongside the seminary at Douai. Foundations followed at Dieulouard in 1608, and St Malo in 1611. A chaplaincy founded at Chelles became the monastery of St Edmund (Paris) in 1615. The English Congregation was formally re-founded in 1619. In 1645, an old foundation at Lamspringe (in Hanover) was taken over by English Benedictines.

There were also a number of nunneries. The first establishment was founded at Brussels in 1598. In the seventeenth century, its nuns founded a number of new communities. In 1625, they founded a nunnery at Cambrai. In 1651, many members of the Cambrai community left to found the Priory of Our Lady of Good Hope in Paris. The Brussels nuns also established another convent at Ghent in 1624, which in turn established another house at Dunkirk.

During the French Revolutionary era, English Benedictines fled the continent. St Gregory's was re-founded at Downside, Dieulouard at Ampleforth. After the restoration of the French monarchy, the monks of St Edmund's re-established themselves in the premises at Douai vacated by the monks of St Gregory, but moved to Woolhampton in 1903. The Lamspringe community was dissolved in 1803; its school was transferred to the newly established Ampleforth. The monks themselves dispersed, but came together again briefly between 1823 and 1841 at Broadway (Worcestershire).

Benedictine nuns also re-established themselves in England. The Brussels nuns fled to Winchester in 1794, finally settling at East Bergholt in 1857. Cambrai's nuns eventually came together again at Stanbrook (Worcestershire) in 1838. The community moved to Wass (Yorkshire) in 2009. The Parisian nuns fled to Dorset, re-establishing themselves at Cannington (Somerset), and finally (in 1826) at Colwich. The Ghent nuns found a new home at Oulton (Staffordshire).[3] The Dunkirk community fled to Hammersmith in 1795, and thence (in 1863) to St Scholastica's Abbey at Teignmouth.

In the century after the exiles returned to England, a number of new abbeys were founded. Communities settled at Belmont (Herefordshire) in

1859, Buckfast (Devon) in 1882, Ealing in 1897 and Worth (Sussex) in 1933. Buckfast was built on the site of a medieval Benedictine establishment by French monks forced into exile. The convent now at Curzon Park (Cheshire) was originally founded at Feltham (Middlesex) as an Anglican Benedictine nunnery in 1868. Its members were accepted into the Roman Catholic Benedictine Congregation in 1921. There are also a number of houses of the English Congregation in America and South Africa.

A database of early Benedictine monks is currently being created. See:

- Monks in Motion: A prosopographical study of the English and Welsh Benedictines in exile, 1553-1800
  www.dur.ac.uk/mim

The archives of the English Benedictines are held in various locations, many of them on the Continent. For an overview, see:

- Marron, Vincent. 'Some sources for English Benedictine history', *Downside Review* 81, 1963, p.50-60.

Many of the archives of the English Benedictine Congregation, as well as the papers of prominent Catholics such as Bishop Ullathorne and Cardinal Gasquet, are held by:

- Downside Library
  www.downside.co.uk/downside-library

For a detailed listing see:

- Jebb, Philip. 'The Archives of the English Benedictine Congregation kept at St. Gregory's, Downside', *Downside Review* 93(312), 1975, p.208-25. Also online, with additions, at: **http://discovery.national archives.gov.uk/download/GB1151%20DOWNSIDE**

See also:

- Jebb, Philip. 'The Archives of the English Benedictine Congregation kept at St Gregory's, Downside', *Catholic Archives* 14, 1994, p.20-36

Brief biographical notes on over 900 Benedictine monks who died between 1585 and 1850 are included in:

- Allanson, Athanasius, et al. *Biography of the English Benedictines.* St Laurence Papers 4. Ampleforth Abbey Library, 1999.

See also:

- Birt, Henry Norbert, ed. *The Obit book of the English Benedictines from 1600 to 1912, being the necrology of the English Congregation of the Order of St Benedict from 1600 to 1883 compiled by Abbot Snow.* Rev ed. Edinburgh: privately printed, 1913. Reprinted Gregg International, 1970.
- 'A list of the English Monks of the Spanish and English Congregations drawn up in 1613', in McCann, Justin, & Connolly, Hugh, eds. *Memorials of Father Augustine Baker and other documents relating to the English Benedictines.* Catholic Record Society, 33. 1933, p.190-239. This volume also includes 'Fr. Thomas Woodhope's obits of Eminent Benedictines', (p.240-59).

For post-Reformation English Benedictinism, see:

- Lunn, David. *The English Benedictines, 1540-1688: from Reformation to Revolution.* Burns & Oates, 1980.
- Hood, Alban. *From Repatriation to Revival: Continuity and change in the English Benedictine Community 1795-1850.* St Michaels Abbey Press, 2014. The thesis on which this book is based is available online at **http://ethos.bl.uk**.
- English Benedictine Congregation History **www.plantata.org.uk/**

An older history, with an extensive listing of Benedictine monks, is provided by:

- Weldon, Bennet. *Pax: Chronological notes containing the rise, growth and present state of the English Congregation of the Order of St Benedict.* Stanbrook: The Abbey of Our Lady of Consolation, 1881.

Bellenger has edited an interesting collection of essays:

- Bellenger, Aidan, ed. *Monks with a Mission: Essays in English Benedictine History.* Downside Abbey Press, 2014.

Benedictine novices are listed by:

- Cramer, Anselm. *The Belmont clothing book: English Benedictine novices, 1860-1920.* Ampleforth Abbey, 2003.

Ampleforth
For the history of the abbey, its school, its parishes and its other work, see:

- Cramer, Anselm. *Ampleforth: The Story of St Laurence's Abbey and College.* St Laurence Papers V. Ampleforth Abbey, 2001.
- Almond, Cuthbert. *A history of Ampleforth Abbey, from the foundation of St Lawrence's at Dieulouard to the present time.* R. & T. Washbourne, 1903.

Colwich
As already noted, this nunnery descends from a continental priory. Its archives are described by:

- Rowell, Benedict. 'The Archives of St Mary's, Colwich', *Catholic Archives* 24, 2004, p.47-51.

A brief history of the Abbey is available at:

- St. Mary's Abbey, Colwich
  www.colwichabbey.org.uk

Douai
Douai Abbey is now based at Upper Woolhampton. For its history, see:

- Scott, Geoffrey. *Woolhampton 1903-2003: a centenary history; the English Benedictine community of St Edmund King and Martyr, Paris 1615/Douai 1818.* Stanbrook Abbey Press, 2003.

Some archives of the pre-French Revolution Abbey at Douai are held, together with additional records of the English Benedictine Congregation. Visit:

- Douai Abbey: the Library and Archive
  http://www.douaiabbey.org.uk/library—-archive.html

For a brief discussion of this institution's attempts to collect the archives of religious orders, see:

- Scott, Geoffrey. 'Douai Library and Archives', *Catholic Archives* 36, 2016, p.76-88.

Downside
A collection of essays on individual monks at Downside is printed in:

- Bellenger, Aidan, ed. *Monastic identities: essays in the history of St Gregory's, Downside*. Downside Abbey Press, 2014.

Downside Abbey.

The English Benedictine monastery at Lamspringe.

Lamspringe

For papers on the history of the Benedictine monastery at Lamspringe, including a list of professed monks and of students, see:

• Cramer, Anselm, ed. *Lamspringe: an English Abbey in Germany, 1643-1808.* Saint Laurence Papers VII. Ampleforth Abbey, 2004.

Stanbrook Abbey

The Stanbrook community, as already noted, was originally at Cambrai, and is now at Wass. The abbey holds few archives pre-dating 1795, although some relevant collections survive on the Continent. For brief details of these and surviving nineteenth- and twentieth-century archives, see:

• Edwards, Eanswythe. 'The archives of Stanbrook Abbey: Gathering up the Threads', *Catholic Archives* 2, 1982, p.3-11.

Teignmouth

The archives of St Scholastica's include some material from Dunkirk and Pontoise, as well as records from the nuns' period in Hammersmith (1795–1863). They are described by:

- Sinclair, Mildred Murray. 'The archives at St Scholastica's Abbey, Teignmouth', *Catholic Archives* 4, 1984, p.31-5.
- Sinclair, Mildred Murray. 'Unfinished Business: Archives of the Former Benedictine Monastery of St Scholastica, Teignmouth', *Catholic Archives* 11, 1991, p.11-16.

Carmelites

A Carmelite house of nuns was founded in Antwerp in 1619; another house was founded at Lier in 1648, and another at Hoogstraten in 1678. The Antwerp community moved to Lanherne (Cornwall) during the French Revolutionary wars, and again to St Helens in 2000. The Lier community fled in 1794, and finally settled in Darlington in 1830. Similarly the Hoogstraten community settled in Chichester; they moved to Baltimore in 1994. A number of papers from both Amsterdam and Lier survive among the archives at Darlington, and fill eight boxes. A profession book begun in 1648 is still in use – and hence excluded from the archives! For details of Carmelite archives, see:

- Harcourt-Williams, Margaret. 'The Archives of the Carmelite Convent, Darlington, and the background in Belgium', *Catholic Archives* 23, 2003, p.47-52.

The chronicle of the Antwerp Carmelites, which includes *vitae* of ninety-five professed sisters, is printed in:

- Daemon-De Gelder, Katrien, ed. *English Converts in Exile, 1600-1800. Vol.4. Life Writing II.* Pickering and Chatto, 2013.

Other Carmelite establishments in Great Britain are listed by:

- Helen of Jesus, Sister. 'The Carmels of Great Britain: a Checklist', *Catholic Archives* 20, 2000, p.38-42.

Dominicans

Like the Benedictines, the English Dominican Province was never wiped out, although evidence for its activities during Elizabeth's reign is fragmentary, mainly consisting of the records of its persecutors, such as prison registers. In 1645, there were only seven Dominicans in England.

Memorial to St Philip Howard at Arundel Cathedral.

Their fortunes were restored by Philip Thomas Howard, a member of a leading aristocratic family, who served as their Vicar for fourteen years. He made recruits among the wealthier gentry, and established a priory and school at Bornhem in Flanders, a house at Louvain, a convent for nuns at Spillekens, near Brussels, a house in Tangier, and a church in Rome. His successors, however, were not so successful. The Jacobitism of some Dominicans did not help. Their continental houses were closed by the French Revolution. By 1850 their numbers were reduced to seven. However, the foundation of Woodchester Priory in that year helped to revive their attachment to an austere standard of observance. By 1932, there were 183 Dominicans.

For a brief historical account of the Dominicans, visit:

- The Dominican Friars, England and Scotland: History of the English Province
  http://english.op.org/about-us/the-english-province/history-of-the-english-province.htm

The archives of the Province consist of the acts of the General and Provincial Councils, numerous letters, and a mass of other materials. Many surviving records were published in:

- Bracey, Robert, ed. 'English Dominican papers, including an obituary roll 1661-1827', in *Dominicana*. Catholic Record Society 25. 1925, p.95-175. This includes an obituary roll, 1661-1827.

For details of individual Dominicans, see:

- Gumbley, Walter. *Obituary notices of English Dominicans 1555-1952*. Blackfriars Publications, 1955.
- Gaine, Simon. *Obituary notices of the English Dominicans from 1952 to 1996*. Blackfriars Publications, 2000.
- Palmer, C.F. *Obituary notices of the Friars Preachers or Dominicans of the English Province from the Year of Our Lord 1650*. Burns & Oates, 1864.

For the professions of Dominican nuns, 1661-1797, see:

- 'Records of the Dominican nuns of the Second Order', in *Dominicana*. Catholic Record Society 25. 1925, p.726-238. Includes professions, 1661-1797.

Franciscans
In 1559 William Stanney and two other Franciscans went into exile in Pontoise. Stanney admitted John Gennings to the order in 1610; he was a prime mover in the foundation of a friary at Douai in 1618. The Second English Province was founded in 1629. During the penal era, there were generally forty friars stationed in England.

The Douai friary continued until 1790, when its members were dispersed. By 1838, only nine Franciscans were left. The Province canonically ceased to exist in 1841. However, new friaries were opened from 1858, and the third Province was formally restored in 1887.

For a fairly sketchy history of the Second Province, which nevertheless includes a biographical dictionary, 1600–1850, see:

• Thaddeus, Father. *The Franciscans in England 1600-1850, being an authentic account of the Second English Province of Friars Minor.* Art & Book Co., 1898.

There was also a convent of Franciscan nuns, opened in Brussels in 1621. It subsequently moved to Nieuport (1637), Bruges (1662), Winchester (1794), and Taunton (1808). The Nieuport nuns founded a house in Paris in 1658. See:

• Gillow, Joseph, & Trappes-Lomax, Richard, eds. *The Diary of the Blue Nuns, or Order of the Immaculate Conception of Our Lady, at Paris, 1658-1810.* Catholic Record Society, 8. 1910.

Biographical details of both friars and nuns are included in:

• Trappes-Lomax, Richard, ed. *The English Franciscan nuns, 1619-1821, and the Friars Minor of the same province, 1618-1761.* Catholic Record Society, 24. 1922.

The Franciscan Archives include chapter registers, 1630–1838. These deal with matters such as appointments, elections, faculties, obituary notices, and the occasional lapse or apostasy. There are also the Procurators' account books 1773–1843. The notebooks of Provincials include much personal information concerning friars; there are also a number of notebooks of the friars themselves, some of which include records of baptisms. The ledger of Baddesley School records fees paid for the education of early nineteenth-century pupils. For a detailed account of the archives, see:

• Order of Friars Minor in Great Britain: A concise history of the Friars in Britain
www.friar.org/our-heritage
Click under 'Provincial Archives' for a listing of the English Provincial archives.

See also:

• McLoughlin, Justin. 'The Archives of the English Province of Friars Minor', *Catholic Archives* 3, 1983, p3-8.

The nuns' archives are described by:

• McCann, Alison, & McCann, Timothy J. 'The English Franciscan Nuns and their Archives', *Catholic Archives* 4 (1984) 52-4 & 59.
• Henry, Germaine. 'The Archives of the Franciscan Missionary Sisters of St Joseph', *Catholic Archives* 16 (1996) p.21-6.

Institute of the Blessed Virgin Mary
The role of women in the church, despite the important part they played during the Elizabethan era, was largely restricted to the domestic hearth. Mary Ward's Institute was an attempt to carve out an evangelistic role for women. It aimed to provide assistance to the domestic matriarchs who had played such an important role in the early decades of recusancy.[4] It also, as already noted, ran a school. For its archives, see:

• The Bar Convent Library and Archives
  www.bar-convent.org.uk/library_archives.htm
• Gregory, M. 'The Seventeenth and Eighteenth Century Archives of The Bar Convent, York', *Catholic Archives* 10, 1990, p.3-7.

Brief biographies of nuns, benefactors, and others are included in:

• Kirkus, Gregory. *An IBVM Biographical Dictionary of the English Members and Major Benefactors (1667-2000).* Catholic Record Society 78. 2001.

See also:

• Hansom, J.S. 'The Nuns of the Institute of Mary at York from 1677 to 1825', *Miscellanea 4.* Catholic Record Society 4. 1907, p.353-67.

Jesuits
There were eighteen Jesuits in England in 1598, and forty-three in 1607. By 1623, numbers had grown sufficiently for a Province to be created

under the direction of Richard Blount. Numbers remained at 150–200 for the next 150 years.[5] The Jesuits are governed by a General who is elected for life by a General Congregation. He is advised by Assistants responsible for a number of Provinces. The Provinces are headed by Provincials who hold office for a term of years. For Jesuit history, see:

- Basset, Bernard. *The English Jesuits from Campion to Martindale.* Gracewing, 2004.
- McCoog, Thomas. *The Society of Jesus in Ireland, Scotland, and England, 1541-1588: Our Way of Proceeding.* E.J. Brill, 1996.
- McCoog, Thomas. *The Society of Jesus in Ireland, Scotland, and England, 1589-1597: Building the Faith of Saint Peter upon the King of Spain's Monarchy.* Ashgate, 2012.
- McCoog, Thomas, ed. *Promising Hope: Essays on the Suppression and Restoration of the English Province of the Society of the Jesus.* Rome: Institutum Historicum Societatis Iesu, 2003.

A playing card illustrating the execution of five Jesuits during the Popish Plot.

The English archives of the Society are held at Mount Street, London; there are also collections at Stonyhurst College and at Campion Hall, Oxford. The collection at Mount Street includes many letters between the Provincial and the General or his Assistants, including transcripts of originals kept in Rome. There is much information on individual members of the Province before the 1773 suppression, and on the overseas missionary activities of the Society in the nineteenth and twentieth century. The Province was divided into a number of 'colleges', each responsible for a specific area, and each divided into subsidiary districts called 'residences'. The archives of these colleges and residences consist largely of financial accounts, and of the letters and reports of individuals. For details of the Society's archives, visit:

- Archives of the Jesuits in Britain
  www.jesuit.org.uk/archives-jesuits-britain

See also:

- Edwards, Francis O. 'The Archives of the English Province of the Society of Jesus at Farm Street, London', *Catholic Archives* 1, 1981, p.20-25; 2, 1982, p.37-45. Reprinted from *Journal of the Society of Archivists*, 3(3), 1966, p.107-15. Also published in Ranger, Felicity, ed. *Prisca Munimenta: Studies in Archival & Administrative History.* Hodder and Stoughton, 1973. Note that the archives are no longer at Farm Street.

Much information is also available in the Jesuit Archives in Rome. These include the 'annual letters' in which Jesuits reported regularly on their activities. The archives also hold many other letters, and much biographical information. See:

- Archivum Romanum Societatis Jesu: The Archives of the House of the Superior General
  www.sjweb.info/arsi

For Jesuit archives worldwide, see:

- McCoog, Thomas M. *A guide to Jesuit archives.* St Louis: Institute of Jesuit Sources, 2001.

A huge amount of information from the Jesuit archives, including many biographies of the Fathers, and notes on many missions, is printed in:

- Foley, Henry. *Records of the English Province of the Society of Jesus.* 7 vols. Burns & Oates, 1875-83. Vol.6 is the 'diary and pilgrim book of the English College, Rome'.

Two biographical dictionaries identify all English Jesuits prior to 1829:

- McCoog, Thomas M. *English and Welsh Jesuits 1555-1650.* 2 vols. Catholic Record Society, 74 & 75. 1994-5.
- Holt, Geoffrey. *English Jesuits 1650-1829.* Catholic Record Society 70. 1984.

See also:

- Oliver, George. *Collections towards illustrating the biography of the Scotch, English and Irish members of the Society of Jesus.* Charles Dolman, 1845.

The addresses of Jesuits were a closely guarded secret in penal times. The earliest known list of addresses is from 1727–34, and includes the names of some gentlemen who provided them with accommodation. See:

- Trappes-Lomax, Richard, ed. 'Addresses of the stations in England served by the Jesuit fathers, 1727-1734', in *Miscellanea 8.* Catholic Record Society 13. 1913, p. 150-189.

Poor Clares
The convent of the Poor Clares at Gravelines was founded by Mary Ward in 1609. The community has migrated several times, and has recently moved from Darlington to Hereford. Its archives date back to 1609, and are described by:

- Michael, Mary. 'Poor Clare Monastery, Darlington: its History and Archives', *Catholic Archives*, 25, 2005, 19-24.

The register from Gravelines is printed in:

- Gillow, Joseph, ed. 'Registers of the English Poor Clares at Gravelines, including those who founded filiations at Aire, Dunkirk, and Rouen, 1608-1837', *Miscellanea 9.* Catholic Record Society 14. 1914, p.25-173.

A convent at Rouen was founded from Gravelines in 1644. Its chronicle, 1644–1780, is printed in:

- Bowden, Caroline, & Kelly, James E., eds. *The English Convents in Exile, 1600–1800, vol.1. History Writing.* Pickering & Chatto, 2012.

Society of the Holy Child Jesus

The Society was founded in Derby in 1846 as a teaching order. Its early work took place in St Leonards on Sea, Southwark and Preston, although later it expanded in Lancashire and London, and also overseas. Its archives include much material relating to its founder, Cornelia Connelly. Journals, ledgers, and day books from the mid-nineteenth century provide much material for the social historian. These and other archives are described by:

• Wickins, Winifred. 'The Archives of the Society of the Holy Child Jesus', *Catholic Archives* 3, 1983, p.38-42.

Chapter 10

OTHER CATHOLIC SOURCES: MISSION, PARISH AND DIOCESE

Official Catholic records from the penal era are scarce. They could be used as evidence against the faithful if they fell into the wrong hands. The exceptions to this rule are the archives of overseas seminaries and monasteries, and of the Vatican, although the archives of the former frequently suffered during the French revolutionary wars, and much has been lost.

As implementation of the penal laws in England gradually eased, and Catholics became increasingly tolerated, a wide range of official Catholic records began to be kept. Parish records (not just registers) are one of the prime sources of information on the later history of Catholic missions and parishes. Diocesan records are also important. A variety of records likely to be found in these archives are noted below. Typical collections of parish records are described by:

- Tweedy, John M. 'The Archives of the Parish of St Cuthbert, Durham City', *Catholic Archives* 1, 1981, p.32-5
- Waszak, Peter. 'The Parish Archives of All Souls Church, Peterborough', *Catholic Archives* 11, 1991, p.31-4.

AD LIMINA REPORTS
Catholic Diocesan bishops report to the Pope on the state of their dioceses every five years. These reports were originally presented when they visited Rome, hence they are *ad limina*, that is, reports presented at the tombs of the Apostles. Since the restoration of the hierarchy, these reports have responded to questions posed by Rome. They are likely to

give information on individual missions and parishes, and may include the names of clergy. No fewer than fifty-five questions were asked in one nineteenth-century questionnaire! Copies of these reports are likely to be found in diocesan archives, and in the Vatican Archives. The *ad limina* reports for the Diocese of Nottingham are discussed in:

- Dolan, Anthony. The Diocese of Nottingham's *Ad Limina* reports', *Catholic Archives* 30, 2010, p.47-69.

CATHOLIC DIRECTORIES

From 1838 onwards, the *Catholic Directory* provides a detailed regular summary of the state of the Roman Catholic Church in Great Britain, listing the dioceses, the churches and chapels and the clergy. It also provides much other information: religious houses, schools, charities, details of prominent members of the laity, etc. For a period, it was combined with a directory for North America.

- *The Catholic Directory, Ecclesiastical Register, and almanac* ....Various publishers, 1838- .

The *Laity's directory* (1756–1839) was an earlier publication, which included obituaries from 1773, and lists of chapels and clergy in the nineteenth century. These directories are discussed by:

- Fontana, V.J.L. 'The Laity's and Catholic Directories', *Catholic Ancestor* 4(5), 1993, p.214-6.

For obituaries in both these directories, see below, p.186.

In the nineteenth century a number of regional directories began to be published; for example: the *Birmingham Archdiocesan Directory* commenced publication in 1882.

CENSUSES

Reference has already been made to the various censuses of Catholics taken by the government and the Church of England. Roman Catholics were also interested in numbers, and census-type information can be found among diocesan and parish records. Statistical information was regularly provided in the Vicars Apostolics' reports to Propaganda from the beginning of the eighteenth century. Their returns for 1773 are printed in:

• Whyte, J.H. 'The Vicars Apostolics' Returns of 1773', *Recusant History* 9, 1968, p.205-14.

More detailed information is likely to be found among parish records. For example, the records of St Cuthbert's, Durham, include three books containing detailed censuses of the parish, dated 1854, 1858 and 1861, all of which include useful genealogical information. The 1858 census includes the dates of first confession, first communion, confirmation and Easter communion, and indicates when a spouse was Protestant. In 1861, ages are given.

In 1893, Archbishop Herbert Vaughan ordered a census of Catholics to be taken across the whole of the Diocese of Westminster.[1] The returns give names, ages (if under 21), occupations and addresses. They also provide information concerning participation in Catholic rites and ceremonies such as confirmation and attendance at mass. The attendance of children at Catholic or non-Catholic schools was noted. Priests were asked 'Is the child's faith in danger?', and 'Is the child in imminent danger of joining the criminal classes?' The returns are now available at:

• Westminster Roman Catholic Census 1893
  **http://search.findmypast.co.uk/search-world-Records/
  westminster-roman-catholic-census-1893**

COMMUNICANT LISTS

Lists of communicants at Easter were frequently compiled. They may be separate documents, but are frequently to be found in registers of baptisms, marriages and burials. In Durham, two books from St Cuthbert's list the names of all communicants between 1824 and 1860. The numbers recorded rose from around 170 in the early years to around 1,000 at the end of the period. The 1838 list for Biddlestone (Northumberland) begins with Mr and Mrs Stourton of Biddlestone Hall, and their fifteen household servants. Their occupations – the butler, the coachmen, a governess, and so on – are stated. One of them, George Simmons, simply described as 'servant', was taking his first communion. Following the listing of household servants is a list of outdoor employees, beginning with the gamekeeper, Robert Grey, and his family, who lived in Biddlestone village. This list gives the names, residences and occupations of another fifty-six communicants. Ann Gutterson, who is merely described as a 'girl', is also said to have taken her first communion.[2] These details provide an invaluable census of the congregation, and of where they came from.

More recent communicant lists may simply identify young people taking their first communion. For such lists, see Gandy's *Catholic missions and registers* (6 vols. 1993).

CONFIRMATION LISTS

Before James II ascended the throne, and the Pope appointed Vicars General, the rite of confirmation was rarely administered in England. Technically, reception of communion should always precede confirmation, but the rule was usually ignored; it was unrealistic in penal conditions. When Bishop Leyburn toured the North in 1687, he confirmed 18,958 people in one summer. For his confirmation book, see:

• Hilton, J.A., et al, eds. *Bishop Leyburn's Confirmation Register of 1687.* North West Catholic History Society, 1997.

Subsequently, mission registers frequently list confirmations. Bishops' visits continued to be infrequent in the eighteenth century, so, when they did occur, whole families might be confirmed. In the nineteenth century it became customary to confirm children at age eight, so mission records of confirmations can serve as censuses of children of that age – although ages are not usually given.

Confirmation books were sometimes retained by Vicars General. They may be found among Catholic diocesan archives. These are frequently statistical documents without names, and are not always useful for genealogical purposes. The records of confirmation tours of the Vicars Apostolic in the Northern District, for example, simply list the places visited, the names of the priests, the numbers of confirmees and the numbers of communications – but no names.[3]

Details of many confirmation records can be found in Gandy (3). A few have been published:

- *The Bishops' Register of Confirmations in the Midland District of the Catholic Church in England, 1768-1811 and 1816.* Occasional Publication 3. Catholic Family History Society, 1999.Bishnfirmations in the London District of the
- *The Bishops' Register of Confirmations in the London District of the Catholic Church in England, 1826-1837 and 1843.* Occasional Publication 4. Catholic Family History Society, 2001.
- Roberts, Frank. 'The Confirmation Register 1768-93 of Thomas Talbot, Vicar Apostolic of the Midland District', *Staffordshire Catholic History* 12, 1972, p.15-27.

CONVERSION LISTS

Catholic priests maintained lists of converts. These, like communicants' and confirmation lists, were frequently written into registers (see Chapter 4). Some separate lists are also identified by Gandy (3). The names on these lists include not just those who were converted from outside the church, but also many lapsed Catholics who had been reconciled. Church Papists needed to be reconciled before they died. Those who had married non-Catholics also needed reconciliation.

Most converts came from the Church of England. Anglican baptisms were accepted as legitimate by Roman Catholics before the nineteenth century. However, a narrower approach began to be adopted in the 1830s, when converts began to be re-baptised. It should also be borne in mind that Quakers who converted needed to be baptised as adults. The following entry occurs in Rev. Monox Hervey's register:

> On the 11th January 1741 … was baptized Sarah Poritt a grown up Woman, a Quaker, of the parish of Liverton, near North Loftus, by J.R., alias M.H. She answered for herself before these witnesses: Elenora Meller, Ann Meller, Marmaduke Langdale, and Thomas Alenson.[4]

Several thousand nineteenth-century converts, with notes which are sometimes of genealogical interest, are identified in:

- Gorman, W. Gordon. *Converts to Rome: a biographical list of the more notable converts to the Catholic Church in the United Kingdom during the last sixty years.* New [10th] ed. W. Swan Sonnenschein & Co., 1910.

For details of an index to Catholic converts held by the Institute of Heraldic and Genealogical Studies **www.ihgs.ac.uk**, see:

• Adolph, Anthony R.J.S. 'Anstruther's Index of Catholic Converts', *Family History,* 17(138), NS. 114, 1994, p. 45-7.

Many other works on converts are listed by Gandy (1).

EVACUATION LOGBOOKS

In the first days of the Second World War, there was a massive evacuation of children from cities where severe bombing was expected. The correspondence of bishops, and their instructions to their clergy, tells us much about this experience. Also useful are the evacuation logbooks kept by Catholic parochial schools. These can be found in both diocesan archives and local record offices. One such logbook is discussed by:

• Davies, John. 'Evacuation Logbooks: St Peter's, Seel Street, Liverpool', *Catholic Archives* 31, 2011, p.39-49.

MISCELLANEOUS LISTS OF CATHOLICS

One of the earliest reports on the state of England compiled for the Roman Catholic hierarchy was written by Nicholas Sander. Part 23 of his report is 'Of the Individual Action of those who have Defended Religion in England'. This is one of the earliest lists of Catholics in Elizabeth's reign, and is printed in:

• Pollen, J.H., ed. 'Dr Nicholas Sander's Report to Cardinal Moroni, n.d [? May 1561]', *Miscellanea 1.* Catholic Record Society 1. 1905, p.1-47.

Two other early lists, dated 1574 and 1582, seem to have been drawn up on behalf of Mary Queen of Scots to identify potential [Catholic] supporters. These are published in:

• Wainewright, J.Bannerman, ed. 'Two lists of Influential Persons, apparently prepared in the interests of Mary Queen of Scots, 1574 and 1582', *Miscellanea 8.* Catholic Record Society, 13. 1913, p.86-142.

181

NOTICE BOOKS

Many Catholic parishes kept a notice book in which were recorded the notices given to parishioners. A good example from Liverpool is discussed by:

• Davies, John. 'Parish Notice Books as Sources of History: St Peter's, Seel Street, Liverpool, in 1929', *Catholic Archives*, 29, 2009, p.34-40.

OBITS

A Roman Catholic obit is a list of the dead who are to be prayed for. Such lists were maintained in many missions, and are listed by Gandy (3).

PEW RENTS

Like the Anglicans and the Nonconformists, Roman Catholics sometimes raised money by charging pew rents. At St Austin's, Birmingham, for example, the annual rent in 1807 was 24s.[5] The chapel at Ugthorpe was partially paid for by pew rents: a seat on the front five benches cost 2s per year; towards the back seats were rented for 1s per annum, and there was a free bench at the back for 'ye poor strangers'.[6] Lists of the occupants of pews, and records of payments, are likely to be found among Mission records.

STATUS ANIMARUM

These are priests' accounts of the state of their congregations, sent in to their bishops. While recent returns are purely statistical in character, older returns sometimes provide specific information about particular families, for example, the names of the lapsed, of those in mixed marriages, and of those whose children were not attending Sunday School. They can frequently be found among diocesan archives, and may also be written into mission registers.

VISITATION RECORDS

Roman Catholic bishops, like their Anglican counterparts, conducted regular visitations of their dioceses after 1850. Records are to be found in diocesan archives, and include replies to the visitation queries issued by bishops before visitation. Replies to Bishop Goss's queries, for example, have been used to analyse the books owned by clerics, and to assess the level of their scholarship.[7]

Chapter 11

MISCELLANEOUS SOURCES

ARCHITECTURE
This book is focused on written sources for Catholic history. However, the architecture of Catholic buildings is also a prime source of historical information. For a brief introduction, see:

• O'Donnell, R.McD. 'Church Architecture as a Primary Document for Nineteenth-Century Church History', *Catholic Archives* 13, 1993, p.59-61.

Many Catholic archives hold architectural drawings of churches. For the Downside collection, see:

• Bellenger, Aidan, & Eggleston, Paul. 'Downside Abbey Architectural Drawings Collection', *Catholic Archives* 10, 1990, p.26-31.

The development of Catholic ecclesiastical building from pre-reformation times until the twentieth century is described in:

• Martin, Christopher. *A Glimpse of Heaven: Catholic Churches of England and Wales*. Catholic Bishops' Conference of England & Wales/English Heritage, 2006.
• Little, Bryan. *Catholic churches since 1623: a study of Roman Catholic churches in England and Wales from penal times to the present decade.* Robert Hale, 1966.

A number of works list the hiding places used by priests:

Boscobel House in Shropshire has a priest hole.

- Hodgetts, Michael. 'Elizabethan priestholes', *Recusant history* 11(6), 1972, p.279-98; 12, 1973-4, p.99-119 & 171-97; 13, 1975-6, p.18-55 & 254-79; 14(2), 1977, p.97-126.
- Hodgetts, Michael. 'A topographical index of hiding places', *Recusant history* 16(2|), 1982, p.146-216; 24(1), 1998, p.1-54; 27(4), 2005, p.473-520;
- Hodgetts, Michael. *Secret hiding places.* Oscott series 3.Veritas, 1989.
- Squiers, Granville. *Secret Hiding Places: The Origins, Histories and Descriptions of English Secret Hiding Places used by Priests, Cavaliers, Jacobites & Smugglers.* Stanley Paul & Co, 1934.

Many other works on Catholic architecture are identified by:

- Evinson, Denis. 'Catholic Church Architecture: a Select Critical Bibliography', *North West Catholic History* 17, 1990, p.48-50 & 56.

BIOGRAPHICAL DICTIONARIES AND PEDIGREES

Numerous biographical dictionaries contain brief biographies of Catholics. Some dealing with specific categories have been mentioned in previous chapters. For Roman Catholics in general, see:

- Gillow, Joseph. *A Literary and Biographical History or Bibliographical Dictionary of English Catholics, from the Breach with Rome in 1534, to the Present Day.* 5 vols. Burns & Oates, 1885-1902. This is indexed by: Bevan, John. *Index and Finding List to Joseph Gillow's Bibliographical Dictionary of the English Catholics.* Great Doward: St. Francis, 1985.

Gillow draws heavily on Dodd's work (see above, p.XXX), which is also continued by:

- Kirk, John. *Biographies of English Catholics in the eighteenth century,* ed. John Hungerford Pollen & Edwin Burton. Burns & Oates, 1909.

In 1590, Lord Burghley drew up an extensive listing of Roman Catholics in Lancashire. This list has been greatly augmented, resulting in numerous brief biographies of Lancashire Elizabethan Catholics. See:

- Gillow, Joseph. 'Lord Burghley's Map of Lancashire, 1590', *Miscellanea 4.* Catholic Record Society 4. 1907, p.162-222.

Many works on Catholic martyrs are listed by Gandy (1). Those who lost their lives during the penal era are listed by:

- Law, Thomas Graves. *A Calendar of the English martyrs of the sixteenth and seventeenth centuries.* Burns & Oates, 1876.
- *The Martyrs of England and Wales 1535-1680: a Chronological List of English and Welsh Martyrs who gave their Lives for Christ and His Church during the Penal Times (A.D. 1535-1680).* Catholic Truth Society, 1985.

A variety of documents relating to the martyrs are printed in:

- Pollen, John Hungerford, ed. *Unpublished Documents of the English Martyrs, vol.1. 1584-1603.* Catholic Record Society, 5. 1908.

For more recent centuries, many obituaries can be found in newspapers (see below, p.191). For obituaries from the *Laity's Directory*, see:

• Hansom, J.S., ed. 'Obituaries from the Laity's Directory 1773-1839', in *Obituaries*. Catholic Record Society, 12, 1913, p.16-231.

Obituaries in the *Catholic Directory* are indexed in:

• 'Lay obituaries in the *Catholic Directory* 1835-1840', *Catholic Ancestor* 8(3), 2000, p.119-27. This is continued as follows: 1841-3. 8(4), 2011, p.160-7; 1844-8. 8(5), 2001, 195-205; 1849-54. 8(6), 2001, p.248-60; 1855-9. 8(7), 2002, p.18-27.

The lives of prominent twentieth-century Catholics are recorded in:

• *The Catholic who's who & yearbook*. Burns & Oates, 1908-52.

CREED REGISTERS

In 1859, the Poor Law Board required Union workhouses to keep creed registers identifying the denominations of children in care. Subsequently, and despite the opposition of many Boards of Guardians, a series of statutes established that Catholic children in workhouses and other state institutions had a right to receive the support of Roman Catholic priests.[1] Creed registers for Middlesex are listed by:

• Gandy, Michael. 'Creed registers', *Catholic Ancestor* 4(3), 1992, p.117-21.

DIARIES

Diaries, journals, and commonplace books enable us to see the day-to-day lives of their compilers. The commonplace book of Thomas Meynell records the realities of Catholic life. He suffered a dozen short periods in gaol before 1627, paid charges of £450 for forfeited bonds, was prosecuted for his Catholic marriage and steadily paid recusancy fines from 1597 onwards. He used various subterfuges to keep them lower than they should have been; by 1631 he had paid £631 rather than the £4,000 due. At the same time, however, he was sufficiently prosperous to spend £800 purchasing land. See:

- Aveling, Hugh, ed. 'The Recusancy papers of the Meynell family, of North Kilvington, North Riding of Yorkshire, 1596-1676', in Reynolds, E.E., ed. *Miscellanea 17*. Catholic Record Society, 56. 1964, p.ix-xl & 1-112.

Many diaries of priests survive in Catholic archives. For example, the diary of Gregory Sharrock, who became coadjutor to the Vicar Apostolic of the Western District in 1780, provides interesting information about French refugees, and the conduct of confirmation services, in 1799. One volume is held among the Clifton Diocesan archives, another at Downside Abbey.[2]

A number of other diaries have been published; see, for example:

- Phillips, Peter, ed. *The diaries of Bishop William Poynter, V.A. (1815-1824)*. Catholic Record Society 79. 2006.

EPHEMERA
The Catholic historian is often reliant on ephemeral sources such as photographs, memorial cards, postcards, programmes of parish events, book plates and even menus to reconstruct the past. All have something to tell us, and all are frequently to be found in Catholic archives. Their importance is discussed by:

- Bellenger, Aidan. 'Printed ephemera and Catholic archives', *Catholic Archives* 23, 2003, p.73-9.

FRENCH REFUGEES
Many Roman Catholics fled during the French Revolution. The French clergy have already been mentioned (see p.158). Refugees received support from the English government, documented in the National Archives, classes T 50 and T 92.

LETTERS AND PAPERS
Much information concerning recusants is to be found among the archives of office-holders like Lord Burghley. Many of his papers are held among the Lansdowne Papers at the British Library. Others are among the Cecil manuscripts at Hatfield, which have been calendared in:

- Historical Manuscripts Commission. *Calendar of the manuscripts of the Most Honourable the Marquis of Salisbury ... preserved at Hatfield House*. 24 vols. HMSO, 1883-1976.

Among these manuscripts there are two extensive lists of convicted recusants, dated 1582 and 1595. They were mainly from the Province of York, and are printed in:

- Talbot, Clare, ed. *Miscellanea. Recusant records.* Catholic Record Society, 53. 1961.

Sir Julius Caesar was the Chancellor of the Exchequer during the most anti-recusant periods of James I's reign. A collection of his semi-official papers concerning recusants is in the British Library, Lansdowne Mss 153.

The Lansdowne papers of both Burghley and Caesar are available in a microfilm collection in many libraries:

- Hawkins, Michael, ed. *Politics and administration of Tudor and Stuart England: Sir Julius Caesar's papers reproduced in their entirety from the Lansdowne collection in the British Library, London.* Harvester Press, 1977.

Many relevant papers can be found among the papers of Lord Ellesmere, who served as Lord Chancellor during the reign of James I. They are now held by the Henry E. Huntington Library in California, and include numerous significations of excommunication from 1601, examinations of imprisoned Catholics in 1593, a list of recusants indicted in Oxfordshire between 1604 and 1613, and much more. See:

- Petti, Anthony G., ed. *Recusant Documents from the Ellesmere manuscripts.* Catholic Record Society, 60. 1968.

Edward Hyde, Earl of Clarendon, was a leading adviser to both Charles I and Charles II. His collection of state papers is now in Oxford University's Bodleian Library. Much material relating to recusants is calendared in the final two volumes of:

- Ogle, O., et al, eds. *Calendar of the Clarendon State papers preserved in the Bodleian library*. 5 vols. Oxford University Press, 1869-1970.

Sir John Bankes was Attorney General from 1634 to 1640. His papers in the Bodleian Library include many relating to action taken against Catholics. See:

- Havran, M.J. 'Sources for Recusant History among the Bankes Papers in the Bodleian', *Recusant History* 5(6), 1960, p.246-55.

The letters and papers of a number of early Catholic leaders are in print. For Cardinal Allen, see:

- Allen, William. *The letters and memorials of William Cardinal Allen (1532-1594)*. ed. Thomas Francis Knox. 1882. Reprinted Gregg Press, 1965. In Latin.
- Ryan, Patrick, ed. 'Correspondence of Cardinal Allen', in *Miscellanea* 7. Catholic Record Society, 9. 1911, p.12-105.
- Renold, P., ed. *Letters of William Allen and Richard Barret, 1572-1598.* Catholic Record Society, 58. 1967.

For Robert Persons, the Jesuit leader, see:

- Hicks, L., ed. *Letters and memorials of Father Robert Persons, S.J. Col 1. To 1588.* Catholic Record Society 39. 1942. No more published.

The letters of many Anglican bishops contain much information concerning Catholicism; see, for example:

- Houlbrooke, R.A., ed. *The letter book of John Parkhurst, Bishop of Norwich, compiled during the years 1571-5*. Norfolk Record Society, 43. 1975.

Robert Persons played a major role in establishing the English Jesuit mission

More personal information may be found in the papers of Catholic gentry families. For example, the Courtfield muniments provide much interesting information concerning the harbouring of a priest by Dame

Joan Vaughan. She faced trial, but was able to secure a mandate from Charles I staying execution of any sentence. The relevant papers are printed in:

- Matthews, John Hobson. 'Papers from Courtfield Muniments', *Miscellanea 8*. Catholic Record Society 13. 1913, p.150-159.

Another example is provided by the Bedingfield manuscripts, which include many letters, a prayer book containing family information dating from around 1590, a memorandum book dating from around 1698, and a census of Oxburgh Catholics 1790–1804. See:

- Pollen, J.H., ed. *Miscellanea VI: Bedingfield papers, &c.* Catholic Record Society 7. 1909.

Stapleton, Langdale, and Constable were all well-known names in northern Catholicism. Their family papers, and those of a few other Catholic families, are now held by Hull University, and are described in:

- Williams, J. Anthony. 'Catholic Family Papers in Hull University Library', Catholic Archives 3, 1983, p.27-30.
- Roberts, Helen. 'Resources for the study of Catholic History at Hull University Brynmore Jones Library', *Catholic Archives* 24, 2004, p.36-40.

The correspondence of a well-connected London bookseller throws much light on late-eighteenth-century Catholicism:

- Blom, F., et al, eds. *The Correspondence of James Peter Coghlan (1731-1800)*. Catholic Record Society 80. 2007.

Many other relevant collections can be identified in the reports of the Historical Manuscripts Commission, and the publications of the Catholic Record Society.

LAWYERS
Acts of 1605 and 1701 prohibited Catholics from practising law. This

restriction was repealed by the Catholic Relief Act 1791. Two National Archives classes list Catholic lawyers in the following decades. The oaths of Catholic solicitors 1791–1813 are recorded in C217/180/5. Catholic attorneys admitted to practice in the Court of Common Pleas are listed in CP10 until 1836.

NEWSPAPERS AND JOURNALS

There have in the past been numerous Catholic newspapers and magazines publishing a wide range of information about Catholics, including news, personal notices, obituaries and other matter. Reference has already been made to the various Catholic directories, and to newspaper obituaries. Gandy (1) gives a summary listing of numerous Catholic periodicals. For a more detailed list of early Catholic publications, see:

• Fletcher, J.E. 'Early Catholic periodicals in England', *Dublin Review*, 198(397), 1936, p.284-310.

For the history of the Catholic press post-1850, see:

• Dwyer, J.J. 'The Catholic Press, 1850-1950', in Beck, George Andrew, ed. *The English Catholics 1850-1950*. Burns Oates, 1950, p.475-514.

Catholic periodicals worldwide are indexed in:

• *The Catholic periodical index*. Catholic Library Association, et al, 1933-66. Continued by the *Catholic Periodical and Literature Index*. Catholic Library Association, 1968- . Available online from 1981 at **www.atla.com/products/catalog/Pages/cpli-db.aspx**

The Tablet, which commenced publication in 1840, is still one of the leading Catholic periodicals; back numbers are currently being digitised at:

• The Tablet Archive
http://archive.thetablet.co.uk
Subscription required.

TRADE DIRECTORIES

Trade directories frequently provide information concerning Catholic chapels. For example, Francis White & Co.'s *History, gazetteer and directory of Norfolk* (1854) includes histories of the two Catholic chapels in Norwich. It is well worth checking trade directories for the locations of chapels and the names of priests. For listings of directories, see:

• Norton, Jane E. *Guide to the national and provincial directories of England and Wales, excluding London, published before 1856.* Royal Historical Society guides and handbooks 5. 1950.
• Shaw, Gareth, & Tipper, Alison. *British directories: a bibliography and guide to directories published in England and Wales (1850-1950) and Scotland (1773-1950).* 2nd ed. Mansell Publishing, 1997.

Many trade directories are available on-line at:

• Historical Directories
http://specialcollections.le.ac.uk/cdm/landingpage/collection /p16445coll4

WILLS

Catholics had to prove their wills in the probate courts of the Church of England if they did not wish to die intestate. However, Catholics who had been excommunicated could not have their wills proved, nor could they act as executors. They had to make alternative arrangements if they could. Those who had not been excommunicated had to be very careful about the content of their wills. They could not leave bequests for 'superstitious' purposes, such as masses for the dead, or the support of Catholic colleges overseas; otherwise their wills might be ruled invalid. Under a statute of 1605 convicted recusants could not serve as executors.[4]

Catholics sought ways around these difficulties, either by disguising the purpose of bequests, or by using a different legal device to ensure that their wishes were carried out. William Knype of Semley (Dorset) left £100 to 'my friend Mr Dowaie', obviously referring to the Roman Catholic college at Douai where his son George had been educated.[5] Dorothy Barnes of Stourton (Wiltshire) made a deed of gift,[6] rather than a will. In it, she gave the whole of her personal estate to three of her friends, unconditionally. When she died in 1727, the deed enabled them to obtain a grant of administration in the Archdeaconry court. However, she told the trustees privately what she wanted them to do with the 'gift', and also wrote 'private instructions' to the 14th Lord Stourton (who was not one of the three), including the request that 'five pounds to be given away for my self and my son John to be prayed for'. The major drawback of making a deed of gift was that there could be no legal comeback if the 'private instructions' were not followed. The trustees could easily misappropriate the funds for their own use.

Both William Knype and Dorothy Barnes successfully negotiated the minefield of anti-Catholic probate legislation. In practice, despite the difficulties, numerous Catholic wills were proved in the innumerable ecclesiastical courts of England and Wales, before the whole system was replaced under the 1857 Probate Act. Some testators did not consider subterfuge necessary. When Sir Philip Constable, Bt., made his will in 1664 he simply bequeathed £40 'to the English monks at Douai'.[7] However, he had suffered severely during the Interregnum, and may have assumed that his legacy would be ignored by the ecclesiastical court.

Most testators' wills were proved in their local Archdeaconry court. They could, however, also use diocesan consistory courts, the prerogative courts of Canterbury and York, and an array of other courts exercising probate jurisdiction. Catholic gentry were likely to use one of the prerogative courts, although the records of all relevant courts should be checked.

Despite the existing law, which one might have supposed would make Catholic wills void, Parliament found it necessary to pass the Registration of Papist Estates Act in 1715, in the wake of the first Jacobite Rebellion. We have already seen how this required Catholics to register their landholdings. It also required them to register their wills, either with the Clerk of the Peace, or in a Westminster court. Many are enrolled on the Close Rolls, now in the National Archives class C 54. They were also enrolled on the Recovery Rolls CP 43, and elsewhere. The requirement lapsed in 1778. For an incomplete list of these wills, see:

- 'Some wills in the Public Record Office', *Genealogist* New series 1, 1884, p.266-7; 2, 1885, p.59-60 &279-82; 3, 1886, p.122-3, 185-7, & 220-2.

Many Catholic wills are abstracted in:

• Payne, John Orlebar, ed. *Records of the English Catholics of 1715, compiled wholly from original documents.* Burns & Oates, 1889.

The names of people who appear in the wills of over 4,000 Catholics are listed in:

• *Lancashire Catholic Wills 1492-1894: index of people named in the wills of reputed Catholics.* CD. Catholic Family History Society, 2010.

The ecclesiastical probate system was complicated, and cannot be described in detail here. For a detailed overview see:

• Raymond, Stuart A. *The Wills of our Ancestors: a guide to Probate Records for Family & Local Historians.* Pen & Sword, 2012.

A detailed guide to the locations of probate records, which identifies digitised collections of wills, and provides a comprehensive list of indexes, is provided by:

• Gibson, Jeremy. *Probate jurisdictions: where to look for wills,* revised by Stuart A. Raymond. 6th ed. Family History Partnership, 2016.

NOTES

Chapter 1

1. The best online edition is *The Unabridged Acts and Monuments Online* **www.johnfoxe.org**
2. Duffy, Eamon. *The Stripping of the altars: Traditional Religion in England, 1400-1580.* 2nd ed. Yale University Press, 2005.
3. The words of Augustine Baker, Benedictine (1575-1641), quoted by Leys, M.D.R. *Catholics in England 1559-1829: a social history.* Longmans, 1961, p.9.
4. Trimble, William Raleigh. *The Catholic laity in Elizabethan England 1558-1603.* Belknap Press of Harvard University Press, 1964, p.23.
5. Duffy, Eamon. *The Voices of Morebath: Reformation and Rebellion in an English Village.* Yale University Press, 2003.
6. Cited in Haigh, Christopher, ed. *The English Reformation Revised.* Cambridge University Press, 1977, p.179.
7. Mullett, Michael A. *Catholics in Britain and Ireland, 1558-1829.* St Martin's Press, 1998, p.9.
8. Haigh, op cit, p.187; Aveling, Hugh. *Northern Catholics: the Catholic Recusants of the North Riding of Yorkshire.* Geoffrey Chapman, 1966, p.34.
9. Bellenger, Aidan. 'Seeking a Bishop: Roman Catholic Episcopacy in Wales from the Reformation to Queen Victoria', *Journal of Welsh Religious History* 4, 1996, p.52.
10. The word derives from the Latin '*recusare*' – to refuse. For its history, see Bowler, Hugh, ed. *Recusant roll no.2 (1593-1594).* Catholic Record Society, 57. 1965, p.viii-ix.
11. Peacock, Edward, ed. *A list of the Roman Catholics in the County of York in 1604.* John Camden Hotten, 1872, p.1.
12. Sometimes known as Parsons.
13. Sulston, Andrew. 'Catholic recusancy in Elizabethan Norfolk', *Norfolk archaeology* 43(1), 1998, p.102.
14. Available in English translation at **www.papalencyclicals.net/Pius05/p5regnans.htm**

15. Paul, John E. 'Hampshire recusants in the time of Elizabeth I', *Proceedings of the Hampshire Field Club*, 21(2), 1959, p.67 & 77.
16. Trimble, op cit, p.137.
17. Peacock, op cit, p.121.
18. Haigh, op cit, p.184.
19. Bossy, John. *The English Catholic Community, 1570-1850*. Darton Longman & Todd, 1975, p.191-3.
20. Dickens, A.G. 'The extent and character of recusancy in Yorkshire, 1604', *Yorkshire Archaeological Journal* 37(145), 1948, p.24-48. The same number was found during an earlier drive against recusants in 1580-82; cf. Aveling, J.C.H. *The Handle and the Axe: the Catholic recusants in England from Reformation to Emancipation*. Blond & Briggs, 1978, p.66.
21. Dickens, op cit, gives this figure on p.29, but 2,454 on p.28.
22. Sulston, Andrew. 'Catholic recusancy in Elizabethan Norfolk', *Norfolk archaeology* 43(1), 1998, p.101.
23. Aveling, *Handle*, op cit, p.66.
24. Bossy, op cit, p.188.
25. McClain, Lisa. *Lest we be Damned: Practical Innovation and Lived Experience among Catholics in Protestant England, 1559-1642*. Routledge, 2004, p.137 & 244.
26. Renold, P., ed. *The Wisbech stirs. 1595-1598*. Catholic Record Society 51. 1958.
27. They are listed in Law, Thomas Graves. *A Historical Sketch of the Conflicts between Jesuits and Seculars in the Reign of Queen Elizabeth* … . David Nutt, 1889, p.135-7.
28. Mullett, Michael A. *Catholics in Britain and Ireland, 1558-1829*. St. Martin's Press, 1998, p.72.
29. Bossy, op cit, p.175.
30. A list of gentry who employed Catholic chaplains is provided by Williams, J. Anthony. 'The Distribution of Catholic chaplaincies in the early eighteenth century', *Recusant History* 12(1), 1973, p.42-8.
31. Sulston, op cit, p.98-110.
32. Steel, D.J., & Samuel, Edgar R. *Sources for Roman Catholic and Jewish genealogy and Family History*. National Index of Parish Registers 3. Phillimore, 1974, p.833.
33. Aveling, *Handle,* op cit, p.162.
34. Ibid, p.124 & 148.

35. Mullett, op cit, p.70.

36. Analysis of the papers of the Committees for Compounding and for Advance of Money demonstrates that Catholics formed only a minority of Royalists in every county; cf. Lindley, K.J. 'The Lay Catholics of England in the Reign of Charles I', *Journal of Ecclesiastical History* 22, 1971, p.220.

37. Sources for Jacobites are discussed by Oates, Jonathan. 'Sources for the study of the Jacobite Rebellions of 1715 and 1745 in England', *Local Historian* 32(3), 2002, p.156-72. For the involvement of Lancashire Catholics, see Blackwood, B.Gordon. 'Lancashire Catholics, Protestants and Jacobites during the 1715 Rebellion', *Recusant History* 22(1), 1994, p.41-59. This includes a list showing the 'Political allegiances of Lancashire Catholic gentry in the Civil Wars (1642-48) and in the Jacobite Rebellion of 1715'.

38. Aveling, *Handle*, op cit, p.269 & 279. For some examples of inheritance claims against Catholics which failed, see Williams, J. Anthony, *Catholic Recusancy in Wiltshire 1660–1791*, Catholic Record Society monograph series 1, 1968. However, the estate of Mary Evans of Wells was claimed by a Protestant relative in the 1740s, on the grounds that her heir at law was disqualified by religion; cf. Williams, J. Anthony, ed. *Post Reformation Catholicism in Bath, vol.1.* Catholic Record Society, 65. 1975, p.47.

39. For Jacobite prisoners, see: Sankey, Margaret. *Jacobite Prisoners of the 1715 Rebellion: Preventing and Punishing Insurrection in Early Hanoverian Britain.* Ashgate, 2005.

40. Vallance, Ted. 'Make Catholics Pay', *BBC History Magazine,* September 2015, p.44-7.

41. Haydon, C.M. 'The anti-Catholic activity of the SPG, c.1698-1740', *Recusant History* 18(4), 1987, p.418-21.

42. Rowlands, Marie B., ed. *English Catholics of Parish and Town 1558-1778.* Catholic Record Society, 1999, p.74.

43. Steel & Samuel, op cit, p.833.

44. Ibid, p.287.

45. Aveling, *Handle*, op cit, p.258.

46. Steel & Samuel, op cit, p.834-5.

47. Norman, Edward. *Anti-Catholicism in Victorian England.* George Allen and Unwin, 1968.

48. Steel & Samuel, op cit, p.829.

49. For the following paragraph, see Bossy, op cit, p.298-301.

50. Rowlands, op cit, p.80.

51. Rowlands, op cit, p.262 & 267.

52. Shorney, David. *Protestant Nonconformity and Roman Catholicism: a guide to sources in the Public Record Office*. PRO Publications, 1996, p.64.

53. Bossy, op cit, p.307-17

54. Norman, Edward. *The English Catholic Church in the Nineteenth Century*. Oxford University Press, 1984, p.7.

55. Rowlands, Marie B. 'The English Catholic Laity in the last years of the Midland District 1803–1840', *Recusant History* 29(2), 2008, p.384.

56. Quoted by Bossy, op cit, p.316-7.

57. Mullett, op cit, p.181-3.

58. Bossy, op cit, p.184-5.

59. Edwards, David L. *Christian England*. Combined ed. Fount Paperbacks, 1989, v.3, p.125.

60. Hughes, Philip. 'The English Catholics in 1850', in Beck, George Andrew, ed. *The English Catholics 1850-1950*. Burns Oates, 1950, p.42.

61. Norman, Edward. *The English Catholic Church in the Nineteenth Century*. Oxford University Press, 1984, p.205.

62. Tenbus, Eric G. *English Catholics and the Education of the Poor 1847-1902*. Pickering & Chatto, 2010, p.30.

63. Norman, op cit, p.151.

64. Quoted by Tenbus, op cit, p.1.

65. Hughes, Philip. 'The Coming Century', in Beck, George Andrew, ed. *The English Catholics 1850-1950*. Burns Oates, 1950, p.20.

66. Tenbus, op cit, p.4.

67. Brooks, Chris, & Saint, Andrew, eds. *The Victorian Church: architecture and society*. Manchester University Press, 1995, p.13; Cooper, Trevor, & Brown, Sarah, eds. *Pews, benches & chairs: church seating in English parish churches from the fourteenth century to the present*. Ecclesiological Society, 2011, p.60. Many of those built between 1925 and 1950 are listed by Gwynn, Denis. 'The Growth of the Catholic Community', in Beck, George Andrew, ed. *The English Catholics 1850-1950*. Burns Oates, 1950, p.425-6.

68. Hastings, Adrian. *A History of English Christianity 1920-1980*. 3rd ed. SCM Press, 1991, p.134-5.

69. Gwynn, Denis. 'The Growth of the Catholic Community', in Beck, George Andrew, ed. *The English Catholics 1850-1950.* Burns Oates, 1950, p.436

70. Cruise, Edward. 'The Development of Religious Orders', in Beck, George Andrew, ed. *The English Catholics 1850-1950.* Burns Oates, 1950, p.442; Norman, Edward. *The English Catholic Church in the Nineteenth Century.* Oxford University Press, 1984, p.130

71. Hastings, Adrian. *A History of English Christianity 1920-1980.* 3rd ed. SCM Press, 1991, p.43.

72. Ibid, p.473-5.

73. Ibid, p.561.

74. Ibid, p.603-4.

Chapter 2

1. Williams, *Catholic Recusancy,* op cit, p.116 & 143.

2. Ibid, p.103.

3. Aveling, J.C.H. *The Handle and the Axe: the Catholic recusants in England from Reformation to Emancipation.* Blond & Briggs, 1978, p.59-60.

4. The following paragraph is based on Gandy, Michael. *Catholic missions and registers 1700-1880, vol.3. Wales and the West of England.* The author, 1993, p.ii-iii.

5. Yet the seculars regularly sought permissions, dispensations, etc., from Rome through the Chapter without any problem; cf. Aveling, *Handle,* op cit, p.198.

6. Sweeney, Morgan V. 'Diocesan Organisation and Administration', in Beck, George Andrew, ed. *The English Catholics 1850-1950.* Burns Oates, 1950, p.121.

7. Norman, Edward. *The English Catholic Church in the Nineteenth Century.* Oxford University Press, 1994, p.77-8 & 145.

8. Ibid, p.75.

9. Quoted by Sweeney, Morgan V. 'Diocesan Organisation and Administration', in Beck, George Andrew, ed. *The English Catholics 1850-1950.* Burns Oates, 1950, p.140.

Chapter 3

1. Both of these are amongst the Rawlinson mss.

2. Collenberg, Count Rue de. 'The importance of the Archivio Segreto

Vaticano for Genealogical Research', *Family History* 12(87/8); New series 63/4, 1982, p.125.

Chapter 4
1. Williams, J.Anthony. 'Some sidelights on recusancy finance under Charles II', *Dublin review*, Autumn 1959, p.247-8.
2. Rose, Elliot. *Cases of Conscience: alternatives open to Recusants and Puritans under Elizabeth I and James I.* Cambridge University Press, 1975, p.28-9.
3. Their names are recorded in Bateson, Mary, ed. 'A collection of original letters from the bishops to the privy Council, 1564, with returns of the Justices of the Peace and others within their respective dioceses, classified according to their religious convictions', in *The Camden Miscellany, 9.* Camden Society new series 53, 1895. For the statistics, see Trimble, William Raleigh. *The Catholic laity in Elizabethan England 1558-1603.* Belknap Press of Harvard University Press, p.26.
4. For the Elizabethan acts, this summary is based on Rose, op cit, p.11-12.
5. Attendance had first been made compulsory in 1552, although it was not enforced during Mary's reign.
6. For a brief discussion of the twelve penny fine, see Rose, op cit, p.16-17.
7. For a different conclusion, based on visitation articles of inquiry, see Kennedy, W.P.M. 'Fines under the Elizabethan Act of Uniformity', *English historical review* 33, 1918, p.517-28.
8. A mark was two-thirds of a pound.
9. Assizes dealt with Gaol Delivery in the counties, but in London separate sessions of gaol delivery were held.
10. Visitation and other ecclesiastical court records are discussed in Raymond, S.A. *Tracing Your Church of England Ancestors: a guide for family and local historians.* Pen & Sword, 2017, chapter 7.
11. Many are listed in Raymond, *Church of England,* op cit, p.112-6.
12. They could also be made when visitations were not in progress.
13. Marchant, op cit, p.140 & 198-9.
14. Cited by Raymond, Stuart A. *Tracing your ancestors parish records.* Pen & Sword, 2015, p.26.

15. Williams, J. Anthony. *Sources for Recusant History (1559-1791) in English Official Archives.* Catholic Record Society, 1983, p.429.
16. Peacock, op cit, p.121.
17. For common law marriage, see below, p.112.
18. For more detailed information, see Raymond, *Church of England,* op cit, p.123-5 & 127.
19. Clark, Peter. 'The Ecclesiastical Commission for Canterbury, 1572-1603', *Archaeologia Cantiana* 89, 1974, p.194. See also Canterbury Cathedral Archives DCb/PRC/44/3 (calendared by **discovery. nationalarchives.gov.uk**)
20. McClain, Lisa. *Lest we be Damned: Practical Innovation and Lived Experience among Catholics in Protestant England, 1559-1642.* Routledge, 2004, p.213-5; Aveling, J.C. 'The Marriages of Catholic Recusants, 1559-1642', *Journal of Ecclesiastical History* 14, p.68-83.
21. For more detail, see Steel, D.J., & Samuel, Edgar R. *Sources for Roman Catholic and Jewish genealogy and Family History.* National Index of Parish Registers 3. Phillimore, 1974, p.901-7.
22. Dickens, A.G. 'The extent and character of recusancy in Yorkshire, 1604', *Yorkshire Archaeological Journal* 37(145), 1948, p.24-48. On p.29 of his article, Dickens gives the number as 2,461; on the previous page he states the number as 2,454. The return is compared with the recusant roll, and the latter is found wanting 300 names of convicted recusants, in Dickens, A.G., & Newton, John. 'Further light on the Scope of Yorkshire Recusancy in 1604', *Yorkshire Archaeological Journal* 38, 1955, p.524-8. Both these articles are reprinted in Dickens, A.G. *Reformation Studies.* Hambledon Press, 1982.
23. Main Papers 29th March 1679 (no.114).
24. Main Papers 23 January 1688/9 (no.6).
25. Main Papers 1 March 1705/6 (no.2249). See *The Manuscripts of the House of Lords, 1704-1706.* HMSO, 1912, p.417-23.
26. Quoted by Steel & Samuel, op cit, p.907.
27. Calthrop, M.E.C., ed. *Recusant roll No. 1. 1592-3. Exchequer, Lord Treasurer's Remembrancer, Pipe Office series.* Catholic Record Society 18. 1916, p.xii. One such list is printed in Joseph Mary, Mother. 'The Bishop of London's list of Essex Recusants in 1605', *Essex Recusant* 2(3), 1960, p.113-27.
28. For the reports of an active informer, see Harris, P.R. 'The Reports of William Udall, Informer, 1605-12', *Recusant history* 8(4), 1966,

p.192-249; 8(5), 1966, p.252-84.

29. For the report of one such commission found amongst the State Papers, see Hodgetts, M. 'A Certificate of Warwickshire Recusants, 1592', *Worcestershire Recusant* 5, 1965, p.18-31; 6, 1965, p.7-20.

30. Aveling, Hugh. *Northern Catholics: the Catholic Recusants of the North Riding of Yorkshire, 1558-1790.* Geoffrey Chapman, 1966, p.214.

31. Trimble, op cit, p.170-71.

32. For a detailed list, see Raymond, Stuart A. *Tracing your Ancestors in County Records: a guide for Family and Local Historians.* Pen & Sword, 2016, p.74-8.

33. Anstruther, Hugh. *Post Reformation Catholicism in East Yorkshire, 1558-1790.* East Yorkshire Local History Society, 1960, p.42.

34. At least, that is what was supposed to happen. Clerks frequent failure to send in estreats is actually mentioned in the 1586 act, which suggests that it was a widespread problem.

35. These rolls recorded the revenues for which sheriffs were expected to account.

36. Bowler, Hugh, ed. *Recusant roll no.2 (1593-1594).* (Catholic Record Society 57. 1965), p.xxi.

37. Shorney, David. *Protestant Nonconformity and Roman Catholicism: a guide to sources in the Public Record Office.* PRO Publications, 1996, p.69.

38. Bowler, *Recusant roll no.2,* op cit, p.xlvi-xlvii.

39. Ibid, p.xxxv.

40. Ibid, p.cii.

41. Described in detail by Bowler, *Recusant roll no.2,* op cit, p.lxix—cv. See also Bowler, Hugh. 'Some notes on the recusant rolls of the Exchequer', *Recusant History* 4(5), 1958, p.182-98.

42. Bowler, *Recusant roll no.2,* op cit, p.lxxx-lxxxiv,

43. Ibid, p.lxxxvii.

44. Bowler, Hugh. 'Some notes on the recusant rolls', op cit, p.188.

45. Trimble, op cit, p.243.

46. Bowler, *Recusant roll no.2,* op cit, p.xliii & cxi.

47. Aveling, J.C.H. *The Handle and the Axe: the Catholic recusants in England from Reformation to Emancipation.* Blond & Briggs, 1978, p.156 & 159.

48. Gooch, Leo. 'The Religion for a Gentleman: the Northern Catholic

Gentry in the Eighteenth Century', *Recusant History* 23, 1996, p.545.

49. Bowler, *Recusant roll no.2*, op cit, p.lxxv.

50. Ibid, p.lxxv-lxxvi.

51. Firth, C.H., & Rait, R.S., eds. *Acts and Ordinances of the Interregnum, 1642-1660.* H.M.S.O., 1911, p.1170-1180.

52. Mullett, Michael A. *Catholics in Britain and Ireland, 1558-1829.* St. Martin's Press, 1998, p.79.

53. Rowlands, Marie B., ed. *English Catholics of Parish and Town 1558-1778.* Catholic Record Society, 1999, p.66.

54. Trimble, op cit, p.194 et seq.

55. Dures, Alan. *English Catholicism 1558-1642.* Longman, 1983, p73.

56. For a discussion of compounding, see Aveling, *Handle*, op cit, p.156-7. Aveling considers the Northern Commission in his *Northern Catholics,* op cit, p.225-33.

57. 'The Northern Book of Compositions, 1629-32', in Talbot, C. ed., *Miscellanea. Recusant Records.* Catholic Record Society Record Series, 53, 1961, p.307-47.

58. Aveling, *Handle,* op cit, p.159.

59. Lindley, K.J. 'The Lay Catholics of England in the Reign of Charles I', *Journal of Ecclesiastical History* 22, 1971, p.209.

60. They are included in the Harvester microfilm edition of state papers; see below, p.103.

61. For tax records in E179, see below, p.99.

62. Steel & Samuel, op cit, p.922; Bowler, *Recusant roll no.2,* op cit, p.cv; Bowler, Hugh. 'Some notes on the recusant rolls' op cit, p.190-1.

63. Accounts from the Interregnum have been microfilmed in *Unpublished State Papers of the English Civil War and Interregnum.* (Harvester Press, 1975-8), pt 5, reels 20 & 21.

64. There is an index to some of these in the British Library, Add Mss 21275-80.

65. This largely supersedes *The names of the Roman Catholics, Nonjurors, and others who refus'd to take the oaths to his late Majesty King George ... .* J. Robinson, 1745. Reprinted John Russell Smith, 1862.

66. Williams, J. Anthony, ed. *Post Reformation Catholicism in Bath.* 2 vols. Catholic Record Society, 65-6. 1975-6, p.51-2.

67. For a detailed analysis of these documents, see Trimble, op cit, p.180 et seq.

68. For a detailed analysis of the surviving records in the State papers and the Acts of the Privy Council, see Trimble, op cit, p.248-52.

69. Lindley, K.J. 'The Lay Catholics of England in the Reign of Charles I', *Journal of Ecclesiastical History* 22, 1971, p.200.

70. Thwaytes, Lance. 'The Barony of Kendal, 1625-1700', in Rowlands, *English Catholics,* op cit, p.182.

71. For discussion of the reliability of the returns, see McCann, T.J. 'Midhurst Catholics and the Protestation Returns of 1642', *Recusant History* 16, 1982, p.319-23.

72. Main Papers 18th November 1678 (nos.21-2); Main Papers 3rd December 1678 (no.40).

73. A volume of letters relating to Gunpowder Plot can also be found in the National Archives, class PRO 31/6/1.

74. For the location of some other county committee papers, see Pennington, D.H., & Roots, I., eds. *The Committee at Stafford, 1643-1645: the order book of the Staffordshire County Committee.* Staffordshire Record Society, 4th series, 1. 1957, p.xii-xiii.

75. Ibid, p.xii-xiii

76. *Acts of the Privy Council of England Vol. 8, 1571-1575.* HMSO, 1894. p.92, 96, 139, 169 & 195.

77. Ibid, *Vol. 42, 1627.* HMSO, 1938, p.280. For a licence which was not recorded in these acts, see Gillow, Joseph, ed. 'Queen Elizabeth's license to Richard Hoghton to visit his brother Thomas Hoghton, an exile for his blessed conscience', *Miscellanea 3.* Catholic Record Society 3, 1906, p.1-3. Registers of similar licences can be found in class E157.

78. Ibid, *Vol. 12, 1580-1581.* HMSO, 1896, p.103.

79. These are indexed for a number of years by Phillimore, W.P.W. *An Index to Bills of Privy Signet, commonly called Signet Bills, 1584 to 1596, and 1603 to 1624, with a calendar of writs of Privy Seal, 1601 to 1603.* Index Library 4. British Record Society, 1890.

Chapter 5

1. For a general discussion of Catholic rites of passage, see Bossy, John. *The English Catholic Community 1570-1850.* Darton Longman & Todd, 1975, p.132-44.

2. For an example of a Marian register with godparents named, see Gibson, J.S.W., ed. *Baptism and burial registers of Banbury, Oxfordshire.* Banbury Historical Society 7. 1965.

3. The validity of Roman Catholic orders was tacitly accepted throughout the penal years; the priestly status of marriage celebrants was never an issue in litigation concerning Catholic marriages.

4. Outhwaite, R.B. *Clandestine Marriage in England 1500-1850.* Hambledon Press, 1995, p.36.

5. Steel, D.J., & Samuel, Edgar R. *Sources for Roman Catholic and Jewish genealogy and Family History.* National Index of Parish Registers 3. Phillimore, 1974, p.839.

6. For the following paragraph, see Ellis, John Henry, ed. *The registers of Stourton, County Wilts., from 1570 to 1800.* Harleian Society publications, 12. 1887, p.20-21.

7. Bossy, op cit, p.134.

8. Gardner, David E., & Smith, Frank. *Genealogical research in England and Wales vol.1.* Salt Lake City: Bookcraft Publishers, 1956, p.261.

9. Steel & Samuel, op cit, p.855.

10. Ibid, p.854.

11. Williams, J.Anthony. *Catholic Recusancy in Wiltshire.* Catholic Record Society, 1968, p.90.

12. A handful of entries are noted by Steel & Samuel, op cit, p.861. For discussion of Roman Catholic marriages which came before the York High Commission, see Aveling, J.C. 'The marriages of Catholic Recusants, 1559-1642', *Journal of Ecclesiastical History* 14, 1963, p.68-83.

13. For these, see Raymond, Stuart A. *Marriage records for family Historians.* Vital records for family historians 2. Family History Partnership, 2010, p.12-14. For their location, see Gibson, Jeremy. *Bishops' Transcripts and Marriage Licences, Bonds and Allegations.* 6th ed. Family History Partnership, 2013.

14. Steel & Samuel, op cit, p.360-61

15. Burton, Edwin H. *The Life and times of Bishop Challoner (1691-1781).* Longmans Green & Co, 1909. Vol.1, p.339.

16. Steel & Samuel, op cit, p.864-5.

17. Outhwaite, R.B. *Clandestine marriage in England 1500-1650.* Hambledon Press, 1995, p.157-8.

18. Steel & Samuel, op cit, p.885.
19. Herber, Mark. *Ancestral trails: the complete guide to British genealogy and family history.* 2nd ed. Sutton Publishing/Society of Genealogists, 1997, p.247.
20. Thwaytes, Lance. 'The Barony of Kendal, 1625-1700', in Rowlands, Marie B., ed. *English Catholics of parish and Town 1558-1778.* Catholic Record Society, 1999, p.185.
21. Bradbury, Mary. 'Burials of Catholic priests in Anglican churchyards: is this a record?', *South Western Catholic History* 13, 1995, p.3-6.
22. Aveling, Hugh. 'The Catholic Recusants of the West Riding of Yorkshire', *Proceedings of the Leeds Literary and Philosophical Society* 10(6), 1963, p.258-9.
23. Steel & Samuel, op cit, p.849.
24. Whitfield, J.L., & Williams, P.E., eds. 'The Franciscan register of St. Peter's, Birmingham, 1657 to 1824', *Warwickshire parish registers & baptisms 2.* Phillimore Parish Register series 46. 1904, p.1-196; 'The Franciscan register of St. Peter's, Birmingham, 1658 to 1830', *Warwickshire Parish Registers: Marriages 3.* Phillimore Parish Register Series 62. 1906, p.1-68. Includes 'reconciliati', 'confirmati', marriages, and 'defuncti'.
25. Weale, J.C.M., ed. *Registers of the Catholic Chapels Royal and of the Portuguese Embassy Chapel, 1662-1829.* Catholic Record Society 38. 1941.
26. For some examples, see Steel & Samuel, op cit, p.840.
27. Rowlands, Marie B., ed. *English Catholics of Parish and Town 1558-1778.* Catholic Record Society, 1999, p.266.
28. Hanson, J.S., ed. 'The Catholic register of the Rev. Monox Hervey *alias* John Rivett *alias* John Moxon ...', in *Miscellanea 9.* Catholic Record Society, 14. 1914, p.313-80.
29. Steel & Samuel, op cit, p.845.
30. Steel & Samuel, op cit, p.869. Rowlands, Marie B., ed. *English Catholics of Parish and Town 1558-1778.* Catholic Record Society, 1999, p.272.
31. Burton, Edwin H. *The Life and times of Bishop Challoner (1691-1781).* Longmans Green & Co, 1909. Vol.1, p.340.
32. Williams, *Catholic recusancy,* op cit, p.92.
33. For the procedures used in civil registration, see Wood, Tom. *British civil registration.* Federation of Family History Societies, 2000.

34. Rowlands, Marie B., ed. *English Catholics of parish and Town 1558-1778*. Catholic Record Society, 1999, p.272.
35. Smith, J.P., ed. *Lancashire Registers III. Northern Part*. Catholic Record Society, 20. 1916, p.131.
36. Ibid, p.69.
37. Gibson Thomas Ellison, ed. *Crosby records: a chapter of Lancashire recusancy*. Chetham Society new series 12., 1887, p.18-20.
38. The Westminster registers in this database are listed by: Westminster Diocesan Archives. Guide 1: List of Sacramental Registers (Baptism, Confirmation, Marriage, Death) **http://rcdowarchives.blogspot.co.uk/p/family-history.html**
39. Steel & Samuel, op cit, p.846. We have already noted that early Catholics seeking to enter the priesthood who could not prove their baptism had to be conditionally baptised before they could proceed to ordination.
40. For a discussion of their refusal, see Steel & Samuel, op cit, p.846-7.
41. Ibid, p.946-55.
42. Foley, Henry. *Records of the English Province of the Society of Jesus*, vol.I. Burns & Oates, 1877, p.64. For proceedings against those who attended mass at the Spanish Embassy a few years later, see Stanfield, Raymond, & Hanson, Joseph S. 'Proceedings against Catholics for attending mass at the Spanish Embassy on Palm Sunday, 1613-4', *Miscellanea 7*. Catholic Record Society 9. 1911, p.122-6.
43. Brooks, Leslie. 'Recusant History', *Local Historian* 15(5), 1983, p.291.
44. For these, see Raymond, Stuart A. *Tracing your Nonconformist Ancestry: a guide for family and local historians*. Pen & Sword, 2017, p.67.
45. Steel & Samuel, op cit, p.979-96.

Chapter 6

1. Beales, A.C.F. 'The Struggle for the Schools', in Beck, George Andrew, ed. *The English Catholics 1850-1950*. Burns Oates, 1950, p.370.
2. Battersby, W.J. 'Educational work of the Religious Orders of Women, 1850-1950', in Beck, George Andrew, ed. *The English Catholics 1850-1950*. Burns Oates, 1950, p.349.
3. Kershaw, Roger. *Migration Records: a guide for family historians*. National Archives, 2009, p.135-6.

4. For a discussion of these societies, with a list of them, see Heimann, Mary. *Catholic Devotion in Victorian England.* Clarendon Press, 1995, p.127-36 & p.195-9.
5. Identified on Discovery **http://discovery.nationalarchives.gov.uk**
6. Only a very brief selection is given here. Many others are listed by Heimann, op cit, p.195-9.

Chapter 7

1. For more on schoolmasters' licences, see Raymond, *Church of England Ancestors*, op cit, p.135-7. Midwives similarly required a bishop's licence, which was not given to Catholics.
2. Lindley, K.J. 'The Lay Catholics of England in the Reign of Charles I', *Journal of Ecclesiastical History* 22, 1971, p.208.
3. They are listed by Beales, A.C.F. *Education under Penalty: English Catholic Education from the Reformation to the fall of James II, 1547-1689.* Athlone Press, 1963, p.72-3.
4. Aveling, *Handle*, op cit, p.221. Numerous seventeenth-century schools are listed by Beales, op cit, p.205, 215, & 230.
5. For its history, visit Kirkus, Gregory. *The History of the Bar Convent.* **https://monasticmatrix.osu.edu/commentaria/history-bar-convent**
6. The evidence from the State Papers, the Jesuits' annual letters, and other sources, is outlined in Beales, op cit, p.209-13.
7. Anstruther, Hugh. *Post Reformation Catholicism in East Yorkshire, 1558-1790.* East Yorkshire Local History Society, 1960, p.30.
8. Marmion, John P. 'The Beginnings of the Catholic Poor Schools in England', *Recusant history* 17(1), 1985, p.69.
9. Beales, op cit, p.92-6 & 107-8.
10. Beales, A.C.F. 'The Struggle for the Schools', in Beck, George Andrew, ed. *The English Catholics 1850-1950.* Burns Oates, 1950, p.365.
11. Gooch, Leo. 'The Religion for a Gentleman: the Northern Catholic Gentry in the Eighteenth Century', *Recusant History* 23, 1996, p.548.
12. Beales, op cit, p.19.
13. Ibid, p.128.
14. Gooch, op cit, p.550-1.
15. Ibid, p.548.

16. For its history, see Beales, op cit, p.182-3.
17. The sixth diary is lost.
18. Beales, op cit, p.70, 166-7 & 169.
19. Norman, Edward. *The English Catholic Church in the Nineteenth Century*. Oxford University Press, 1984, p.178.
20. Rowlands, Marie B. 'The English Catholic Laity in the last years of the Midland District, 1803-1840', *Recusant History* 29(2), 2008, p.394.
21. Ibid, p.395.
22. For earlier work amongst the poor, see Kitching, J. 'The Catholic Poor Schools 1800-1845', *Journal of Educational Administration and History* 1(2), 1969, p.1-8; 2(1), 1969, p.1-12.
23. Tenbus, Eric G. *English Catholics and the Education of the Poor 1847-1902*. Pickering & Chatto, 2010, p.15.
24. Ibid p.41-2.
25. Beales, 'The Struggle for the Schools', op cit, p.372.
26. Battersby, W.J. 'Educational work of the Religious Orders of Women, 1850-1950', in Beck, George Andrew, ed. *The English Catholics 1850-1950.* Burns Oates, 1950, p.359.

Chapter 8

1. For sources, see Connelly, Roland. 'A Survey of Sources for Information on the eighty-five martyrs', *Catholic Archives* 8, 1988, p.3-12.
2. Steel & Samuel, op cit, p.803.
3. Duffy, Eamon. *The Voices of Morebath: Reformation & Rebellion in an English Village.* Yale University Press, 2001.
4. McGrath, Patrick, & Rowe, Joy. 'Anstruther analysed: the Elizabethan Seminary priests', *Recusant History* 18, 1986, p.2. See also McGrath, Patrick. 'Elizabethan Catholicism: a reconsideration', *Journal of ecclesiastical history* 35(3), 1984, p.424-5.
5. Aveling, J.C.H. *The Handle and the Axe: the Catholic recusants in England from Reformation to Emancipation*. Blond & Briggs, 1978, p.59 & 61.
6. Ibid, p.64.
7. For the following numbers, see Bossy, op cit, p.216-7 & 279. But see McGrath & Rowe, op cit.
8. These are Bossy's estimates, cf. p.223.

9. Bossy, op cit, p.356-7.
10. Bossy, op cit, p.201.
11. Aveling, *Handle,* op cit, p.196-7.
12. Norman, Edward. *The English Catholic Church in the Nineteenth Century.* Oxford University Press, 1984, p.185-6.

Chapter 9

1. Aveling, *Handle*, op cit, p.98-9.
2. Cruise, Edward. 'The Development of Religious Orders', in Beck, George Andrew, ed. *The English Catholics 1850-1950.* Burns Oates, 1950, p.442.
3. Many original sources, lists of nuns, and a 'genealogical tables of some of the principal families connected with our monastery' are printed in *Annals of the English Benedictines of Ghent, now at St Mary's Abbey, Oulton in Staffordshire.* Printed Privately, 1894. See also above, p.XXX.
4. Bossy, John. *The English Catholic Community, 1570-1850.* Darton Longman & Todd, 1975, p.160.
5. Ibid, p.209.

Chapter 10

1. He had conducted a similar survey in 1884-5 when he was Bishop of Salford; cf. Norman, Edward. *The English Catholic Church in the Nineteenth Century.* Oxford University Press, 1984, p.364-5.
2. Hanson, Joseph S., ed. 'The registers of Biddleston Hall, Alwinton, Northumberland, the seat if the Selby family', in *Miscellanea, IX.* Catholic Record Society, 14. 1914, p.292-4.
3. Steel & Samuel, op cit, p.897.
4. Monox Hervey's register, op cit, p.355.
5. Rowlands, Marie B. 'The English Catholic Laity in the last years of the Midland District, 1803-1840', *Recusant History* 29(2), 2008, p.385.
6. Leys, M.D.R. *Catholics in England 1559-1829: a social history.* Longmans, 1961, p.146.
7. Doyle, P. 'The Education and Training of Roman Catholic Priests in nineteenth-century England', *Journal of Ecclesiastical History* 30(3), 1979, p.215-8.

Chapter 11

1. Bennett, John. 'The Care of the Poor', in Beck, George Andrew, ed. *The English Catholics 1850-1950.* Burns Oates, 1950, p.561-2.
2. Bellenger, Aidan. 'Seeking a Bishop: Roman Catholic Episcopacy in Wales from the Reformation to Queen Victoria', *Journal of Welsh Religious History* 4, 1996, p.56.
3. Kershaw, Roger. *Migration Records: a guide for Family Historians.* National Archives, 2009, p.69-70.
4. Swinburne, op cit, p.312.
5. Williams, J. Anthony. *Catholic Recusancy in Wiltshire, 1660-1791.* Catholic Record Society Monograph Series 1, 1968, p.200.
6. Wiltshire & Swindon History Centre P1/B/939; P1/7Reg/177B
7. 'Documents at Everingham', in *Miscellanea* 4. Catholic Record Society 4. 1907, p.269.

SUBJECT INDEX

PERSONAL NAME INDEX